A-Z TAUNTON

G000112091

CONTENT

Inde
Villa
sele

REFERENCE

Motorway	**M5**	
A Road	A38	
B Road	B3170	
Dual Carriageway		
One-way Street Traffic flow on A roads is indicated by a heavy line on the drivers' left.		
Restricted Access		
Pedestrianized Road		
Track & Footpath		
Residential Walkway		
Railway	Level Crossing / Tunnel — Heritage Station — Station	
Built-up Area		
Posttown Boundary		
Postcode Boundary		
Map Continuation	12	

Car Park Selected	P
Church or Chapel	†
Fire Station	■
Hospital	H
House Numbers A & B Roads only	218 17
Information Centre	i
National Grid Reference	320
Police Station	▲
Post Office	★
Toilet	▽
with facilities for the disabled	♿
Educational Establishment	
Hospital or Hospice	
Industrial Building	
Leisure or Recreational Facility	
Place of Interest	
Public Building	
Shopping Centre or Market	
Other Selected Buildings	

Scale

1:15,840

| 0 | ¼ | ½ Mile |
| 0 | 250 | 500 | 750 Metres |

4 inches (10.16 cm) to 1 mile
6.31 cm to 1km

Copyright of Geographers' A-Z Map Company Limited

Head Office :
Fairfield Road, Borough Green, Sevenoaks, Kent TN15 8PP
Tel: 01732 781000 (General Enquiries & Trade Sales)
Showrooms :
44 Gray's Inn Road, London WC1X 8HX
Tel: 020 7440 9500 (Retail Sales)
www.a-zmaps.co.uk

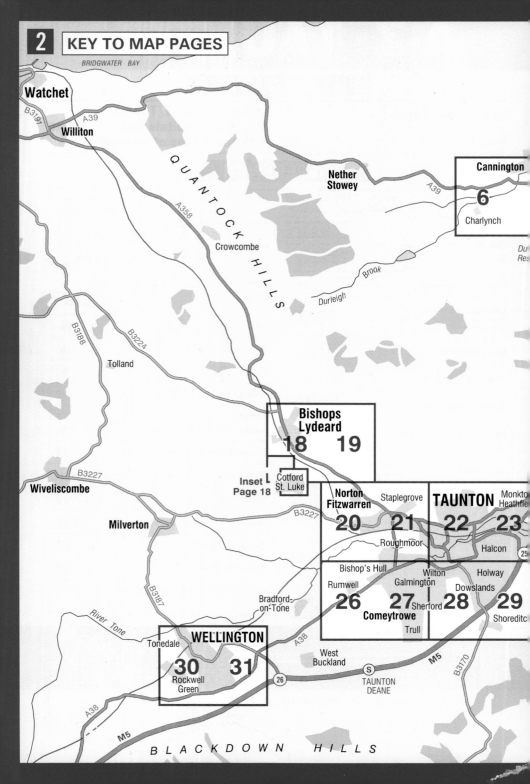

BRIDGWATER BAY

Watchet

Williton

A39

B319?

A358

QUANTOCK HILLS

Crowcombe

Nether
Stowey

A39

Cannington

6

Charlynch

Du
Res

Brook

Durleigh

B3188

B3224

Tolland

Bishops
Lydeard

18 **19**

B3227

Wiveliscombe

Inset
Page 18

L

Cotford
St. Luke

B3227

Norton
Fitzwarren

Staplegrove

TAUNTON

Monkto
Heathfie

Milverton

20 **21**

22 **23**

Roughmoor

Halcon

25

Bishop's Hull

Wilton

Holway

B3187

Rumwell

Galmington

Dowslands

Bradford-
on-Tone

26 **27**

Sherford

28 **29**

River Tone

Comeytrowe

Shoreditc

Tonedale

WELLINGTON

A38

Trull

30 **31**

Rockwell
Green

West
Buckland

M5

B3170

A38

26

S

TAUNTON
DEANE

M5

BLACKDOWN HILLS

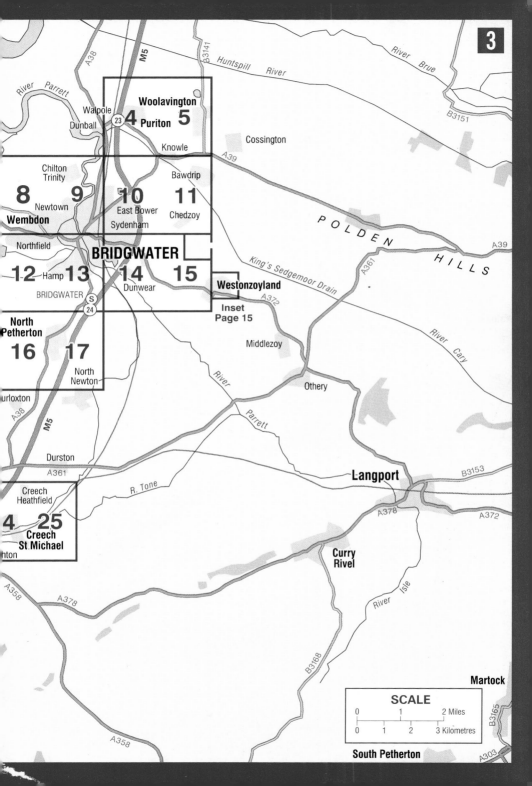

River Brue

River Parrett

A38

M5

B3141

Huntspill River

B3151

Woolavington

Walpole

23 **4** **Puriton** **5**

Dunball

Knowle

Cossington

A39

Chilton Trinity

Bawdrip

8 **9** **10** **11**

Newtown

East Bower

Chedzoy

Wembdon

Sydenham

Northfield

POLDEN

BRIDGWATER

A361

HILLS

A39

King's Sedgemoor Drain

12 Hamp **13** **14** **15**

Dunwear

BRIDGWATER

S

Westonzoyland

A372

24

Inset Page 15

North Petherton

River Cary

Middlezoy

16 **17**

North Newton

Othery

urloxton

River

A38

M5

Parrett

Durston

Langport

A361

B3153

R. Tone

Creech Heathfield

A378

A372

4 **25**

Creech St.Michael

nton

Curry Rivel

A358

A378

River Isle

B3168

Martock

A358

B3165

South Petherton

A303

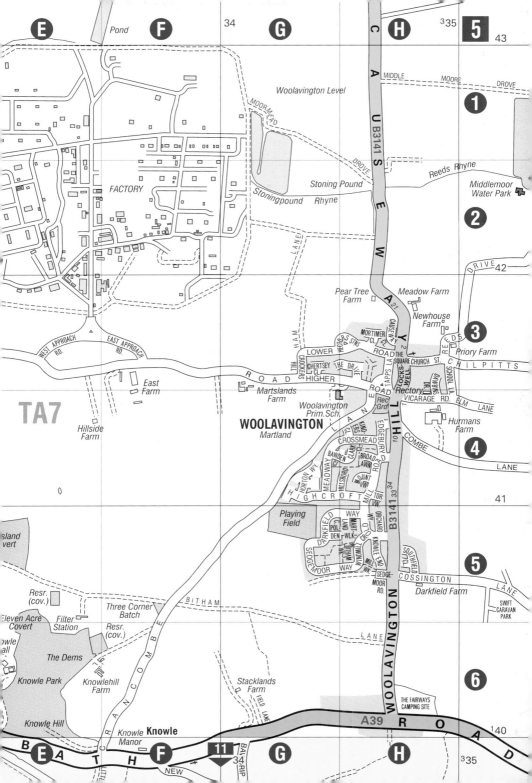

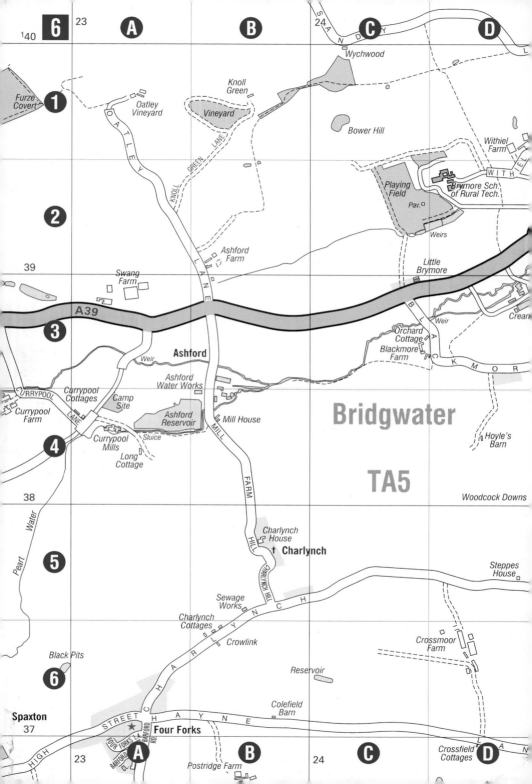

A B C D

1

Furze Covert

Oatley Vineyard

Knoll Green

Vineyard

Wychwood

Bower Hill

Withiel Farm

SANDY

2

OATLEY LANE

KNOLL GREEN LANE

Playing Field

Brymore Sch. of Rural Tech.

Pav.

WITH

39

Swang Farm

Ashford Farm

Weirs

Little Brymore

3

A39

Weir

Ashford

Orchard Cottage

Blackmore Farm

Weir

BLACKMOR

Crean

Bridgwater

Ashford Water Works

Mill House

CURRYPOOL

Currypool Cottages

Camp Site

Ashford Reservoir

4

Currypool Farm

CURRYPOOL LANE

Currypool Mills

Sluice

Long Cottage

MILL FARM HILL

TA5

Woodcock Downs

Hoyle's Barn

38

5

Peart Water

Charlynch House

† Charlynch

Steppes House

CHARLYNCH HILL

Sewage Works

Charlynch Cottages

Crowlink

CHARLYNCH

Reservoir

Crossmoor Farm

Black Pits

6

Colefield Barn

Crossfield Cottages

Spaxton

37

HIGH STREET

BARFORD RD

FOUR FORKS LA

BARFORD CL

★

Four Forks

CHAYNE LANE

A B 24 C D

23 Postridge Farm

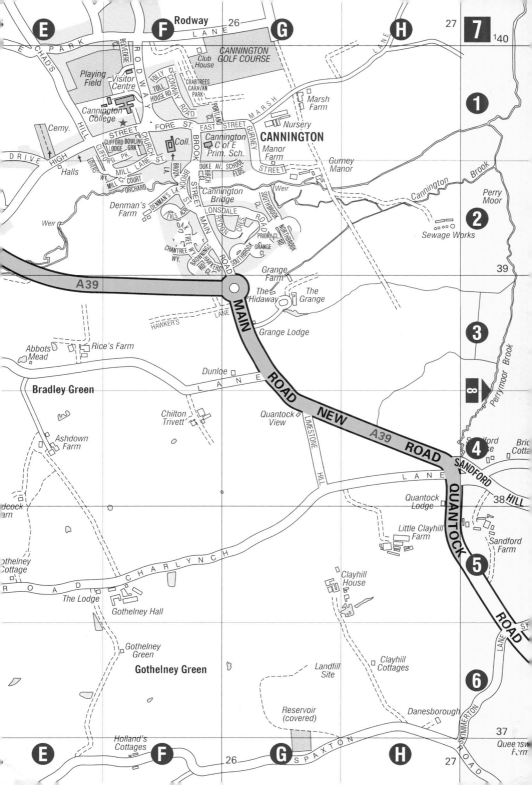

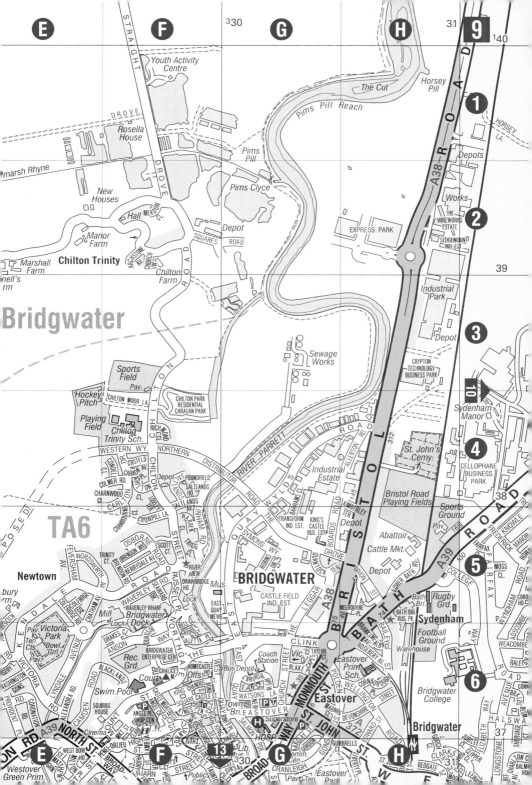

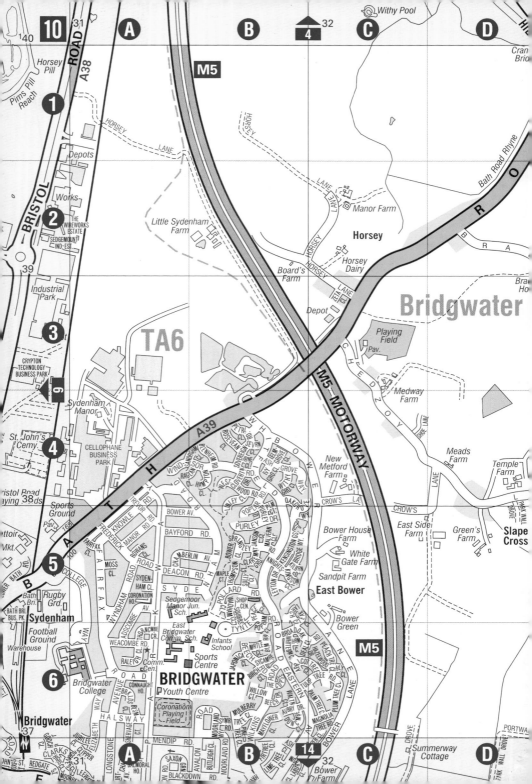

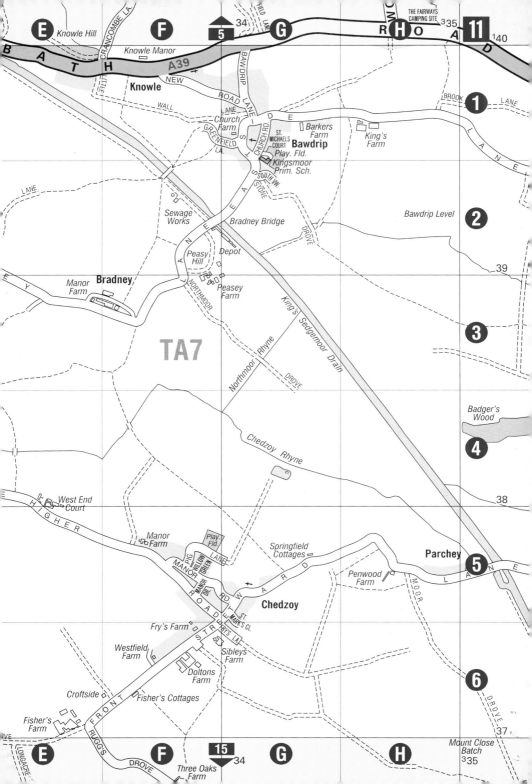

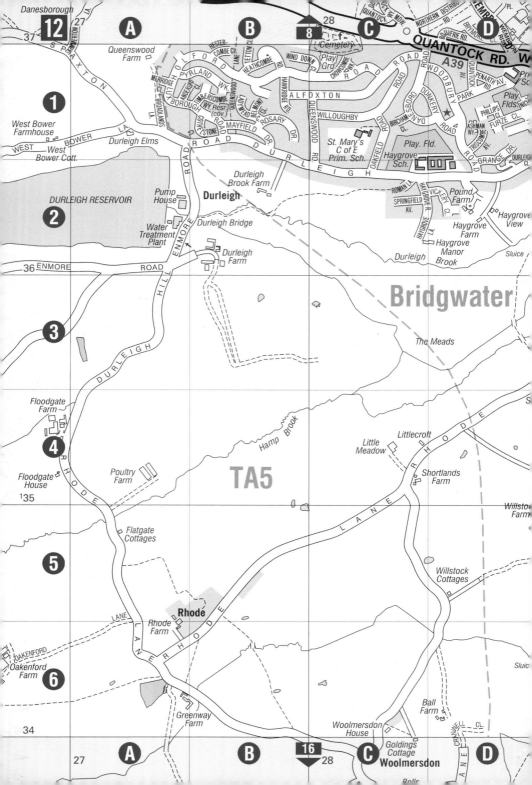

12

Danesborough
27
37

Ⓐ Ⓑ Ⓒ Ⓓ

28
8

QUANTOCK RD. W
A39

NORTHERN DISTRICT RD.
QUANTOCK MDW.
BOUVERIE RD.
BREMORE RD.
EMBA
PL.

❶

Queenswood Farm

Cemetery
Play Gro.
CRONCOMBE CL.
WIND DOWN CL.
Play Gr.

HESTER-COMBE CL.
HEATHCOMBE
TETTON CL.
LANE
HOLFORD
PYRLAND
WK.
HAWKRIDGE RD.
ALFOXTON
QUEENSWOOD
WILLOUGHBY
DR.
ROAD
ROAD
WOODBURY
PARK
QUANTOCK RD.
PENARTH AV.
Play Flds.

MERRIDGE CL.
KILVE CL.
NIDON
BROOMLANDS
HILL
BOROUGH
BICKNOLLER
WY. Resr. (cov.)
BELMONT
ROAD
MAYFIELD
ROSARY
DR.
OAKFIELD
ROAD
BIRCHAM RD.
DANESBORO RD.
DUNKERY
ROAD
IRISCOMBE RD.
ASHMAN WY.
PHILLIPS CL.
FURZE CL.
Pri Sch.

❷

West Bower Farmhouse
WEST
BOWER
LA.
West Bower Cott.
Durleigh Elms
ROAD
DURLEIGH
ROAD

HILL
ENMORE
Pump House
Water Treatment Plant

Durleigh
Durleigh Brook Farm
Durleigh Bridge
ROMAN LA.
SPRINGFIELD AV.
HAYGROVE LA.
VICKERY CL.
St. Mary's C of E Prim. Sch.
Play. Fld.
Haygrove Sch.
GRANGE DR.
DURLEIGH CL.
Pound Farm
Haygrove View
Haygrove Farm
Haygrove Manor Brook
Durleigh
Sluice

DURLEIGH RESERVOIR

36 ENMORE ROAD
Durleigh Farm

❸

DURLEIGH

Bridgwater

The Meads

❹

Floodgate Farm
Floodgate House
135
Poultry Farm
RHODE

Hamp Brook

TA5

Little Meadow
Littlecroft
RHODE
LANE
Shortlands Farm

Willsto Farm

❺

Flatgate Cottages

Willstock Cottages

❻

OAKENFORD
Oakenford Farm
LANE
Rhode
Rhode Farm
RHODE
LANE

Ball Farm
Sluic

34
27

Ⓐ Ⓑ Ⓒ Ⓓ

Greenway Farm
16
28
Woolmersdon House
Goldings Cottage
Woolmersdon
CRANWELL CL.
LANE

Rolls

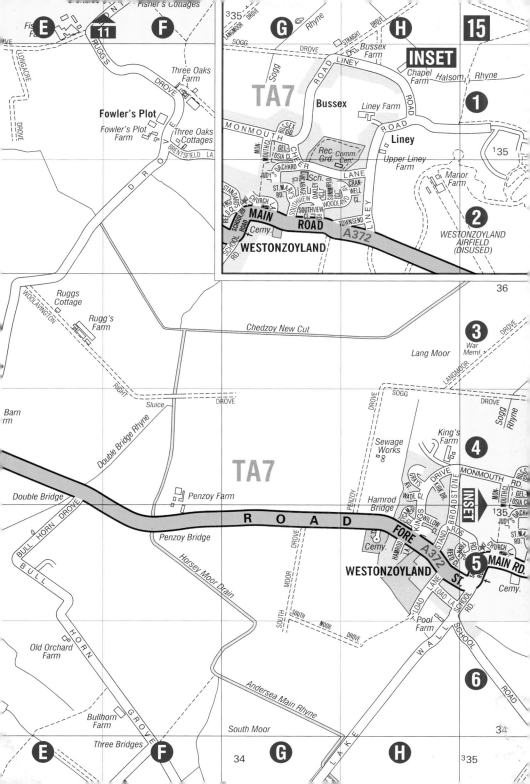

E **11** **F**

Fisher's Cottages

Three Oaks Farm

Fowler's Plot

Fowler's Plot Farm

Three Oaks Cottages

BRENTSFIELD LA.

LONGACRE DROVE

DROVE

RUGG'S DROVE

G Rhyne **H**

LANGMOOR DROVE
SOGG DROVE

335

straight drove

Bussex Farm

DROVE

INSET

Chapel Farm
Halsom Rhyne

1

Sogg

MONMOUTH

Bussex

TA7

GEL JOSIA CL.
SEX. BLDG.
MON.
MOUTH CL.
CHEDZOY
ORCHARD
Sch.
SOUTHVIEW RD.
JUDY
ST.MA'S RD.
VICARAGE CL.
OAKLEY CL.
SUMMERFLD.

Rec. Grd.
Comm. Cent.

LANE

Liney Farm

ROAD

ROAD

Liney

Upper Liney Farm

CRANWELL CL.
WOODLAND CL.
SOUTHVIEW CL.

Manor Farm

135

2

Liney

TOWNSEND
ROAD

MAIN ROAD

CHURCH
RED
STANDARD
SCHOOL ROAD

Cemy.

SCHOOL RD.

WESTONZOYLAND

A372

WESTONZOYLAND AIRFIELD (DISUSED)

36

Ruggs Cottage

WOOLAVINGTON

Rugg's Farm

Chedzoy New Cut

Lang Moor

War Meml.

3

LANGMOOR DROVE

DROVE

Sogg Rhyne

RIGHT DROVE

Sluice

DROVE

TA7

Barn rm

Double Bridge Rhyne

SOGG

DROVE

DROVE

Sewage Works

King's Farm

MONMOUTH

4

135

Double Bridge

Penzoy Farm

R O A D

BULL HORN DROVE

Penzoy Bridge

Horsey Moor Drain

PENZOY DROVE

GRAYS AV.

DRIVE

KIRK DR.

WADE CL.

Hamrod Bridge

KINGWILLOW

SYCAMORE

BROADSTONE

MON.
MOUTH CL.
GEL
JOSIA CL.
ORCHARD
JUDY
ST.MA'S
CHURCH

INSET

135

BULL HORN GROVE

Old Orchard Farm

SOUTH MOOR DROVE

SOUTH

MOOR DROVE

Cemy.

HAMROD
STANDARD RD.
RED CL.

FORE ST.

A372

WESTONZOYLAND

MAIN RD.

5

Cemy.

LOAD LANE

LOAD LA.

SCHOOL RD.

Pool Farm

6

Bullhorn Farm

Three Bridges

Andersea Main Rhyne

South Moor

WALL

LAKE

SCHOOL ROAD

E **F** 34 **G** **H** 335

34

335

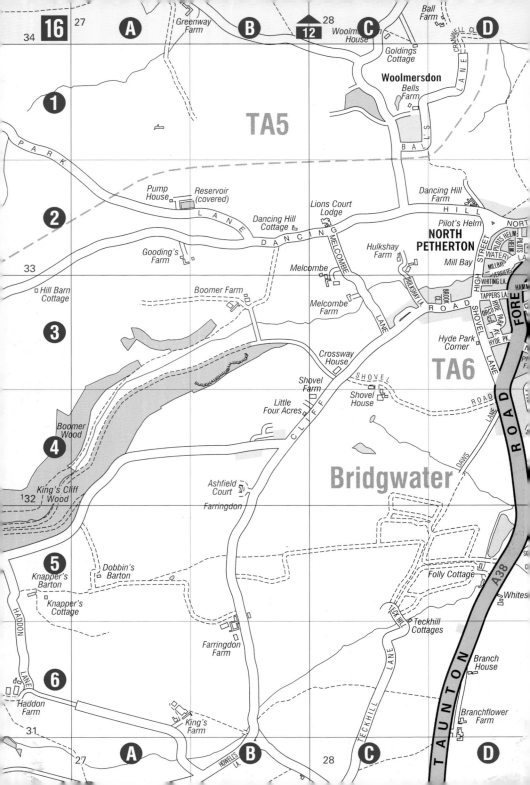

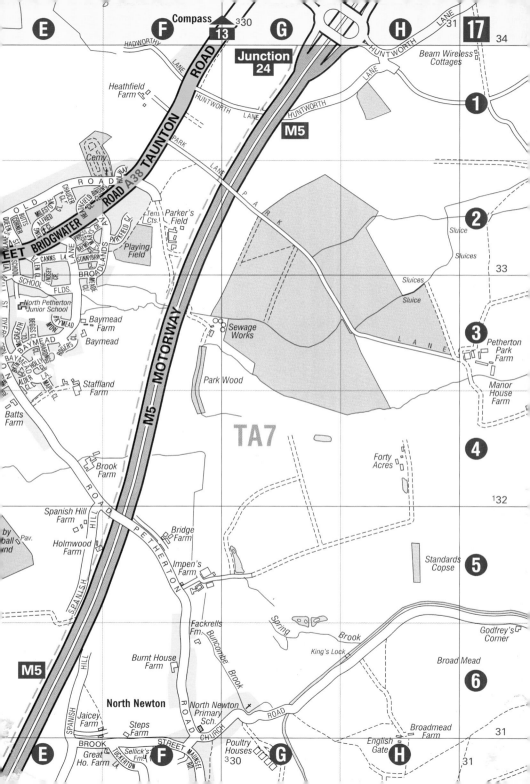

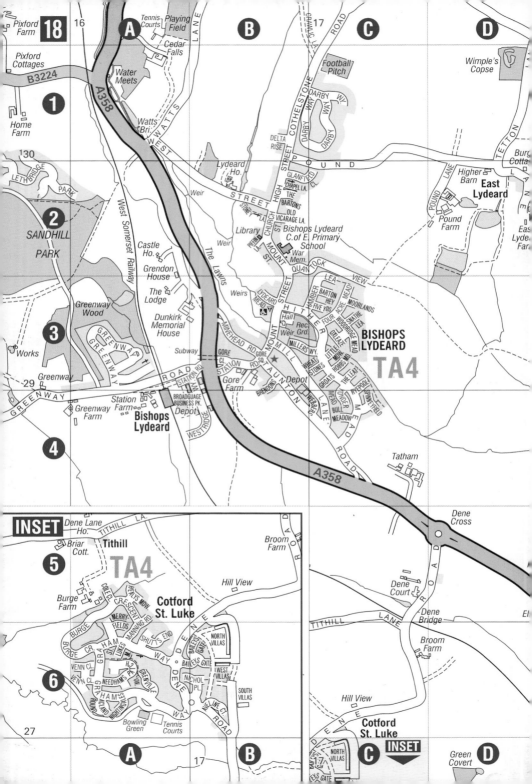

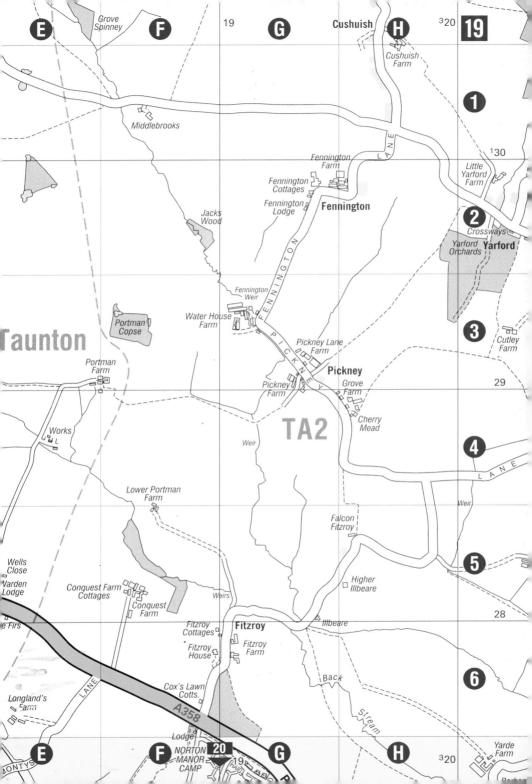

1

Grove
Spinney

Middlebrooks

Cushuish
Farm

¹30

Little
Yarford
Farm

Fennington
Farm

Fennington
Cottages

Fennington   **Fennington**
Lodge

Jacks
Wood

2

Crossways

Yarford
Orchards   **Yarford**

Fennington
Weir

FENNINGTON

Taunton

Portman
Copse

Water House
Farm

PICKNEY

Pickney Lane
Farm

3

Cutley
Farm

Portman
Farm

Pickney
Farm

Pickney

Grove
Farm

29

Works

TA2

Cherry
Mead

4

L A N E

Weir

Lower Portman
Farm

Weir

Falcon
Fitzroy

5

Wells
Close

Warden
Lodge

Conquest Farm
Cottages

Conquest
Farm

Weirs

Higher
Illbeare

28

e Firs

Fitzroy
Cottages   **Fitzroy**

Illbeare

6

Longland's
Farm

Fitzroy
House

Fitzroy
Farm

Cox's Lawn
Cotts.

Back

A358

Stream

Lodge

Yarde
Farm

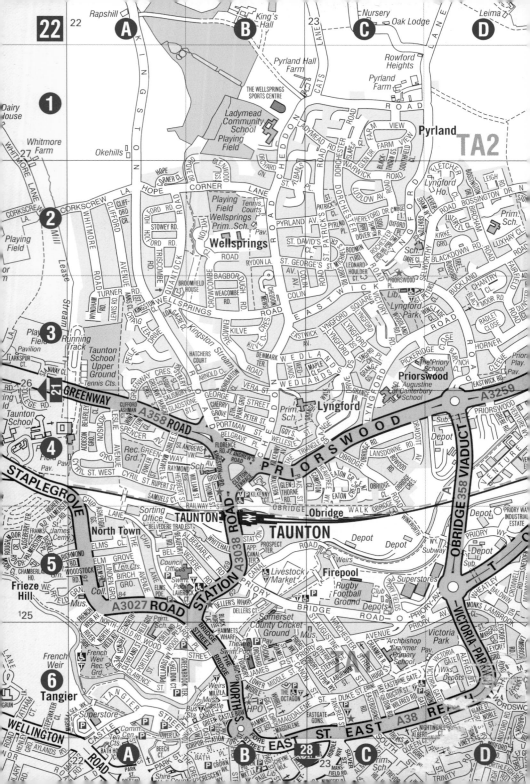

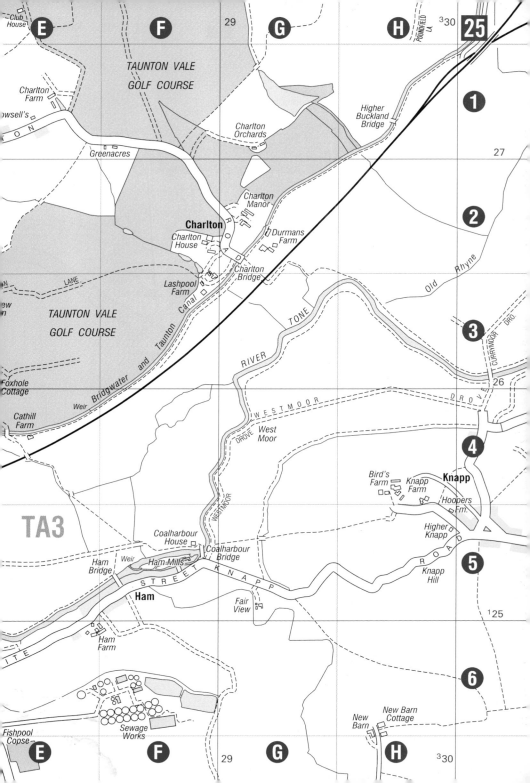

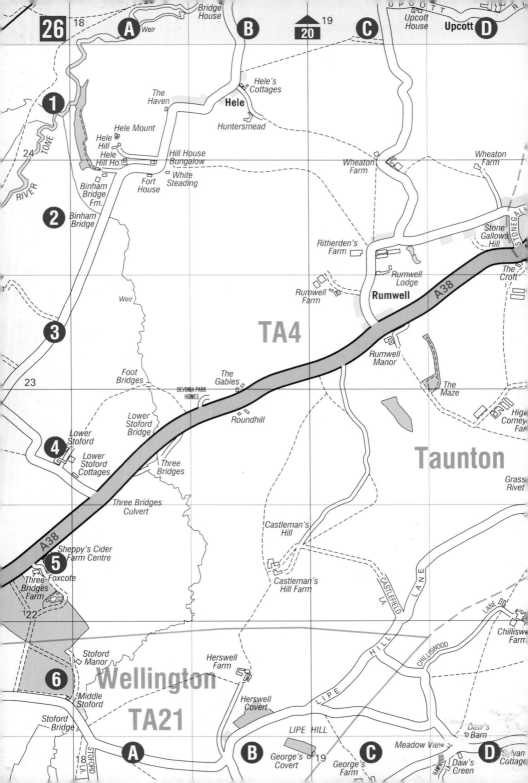

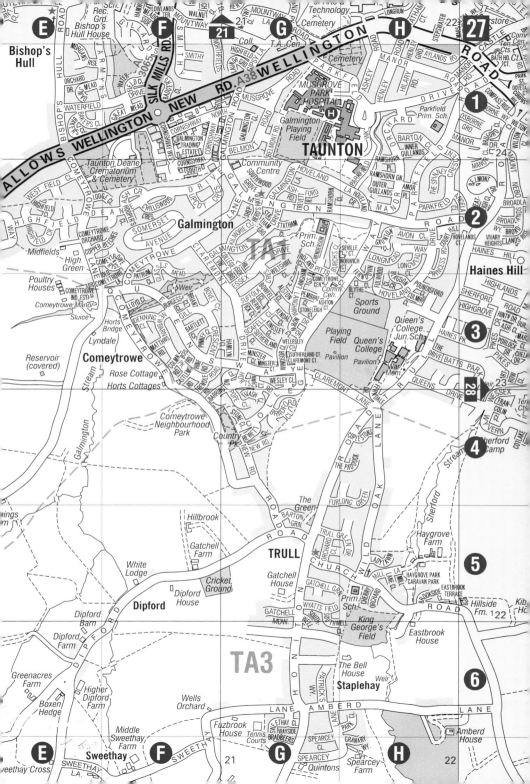

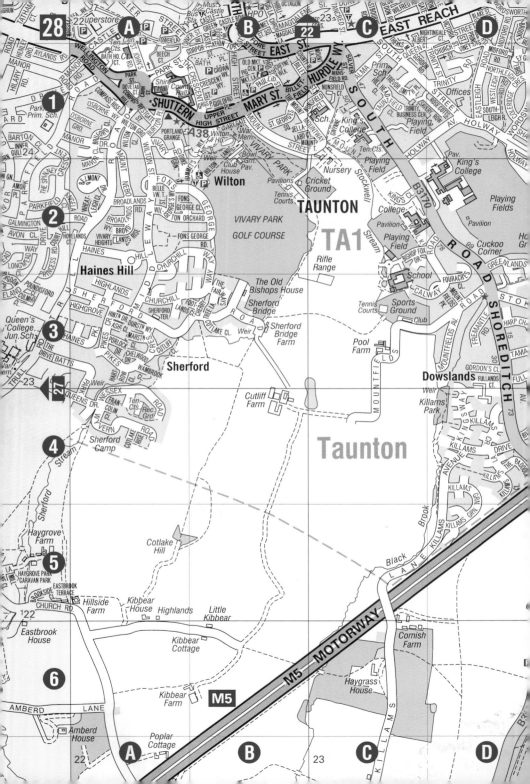

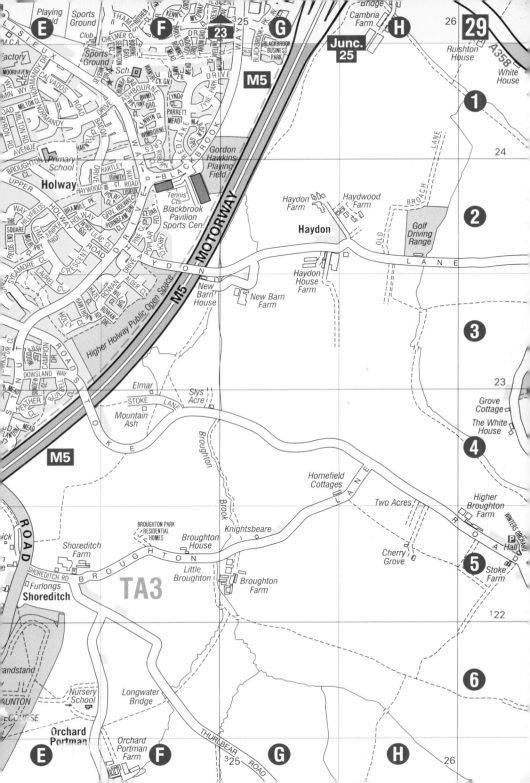

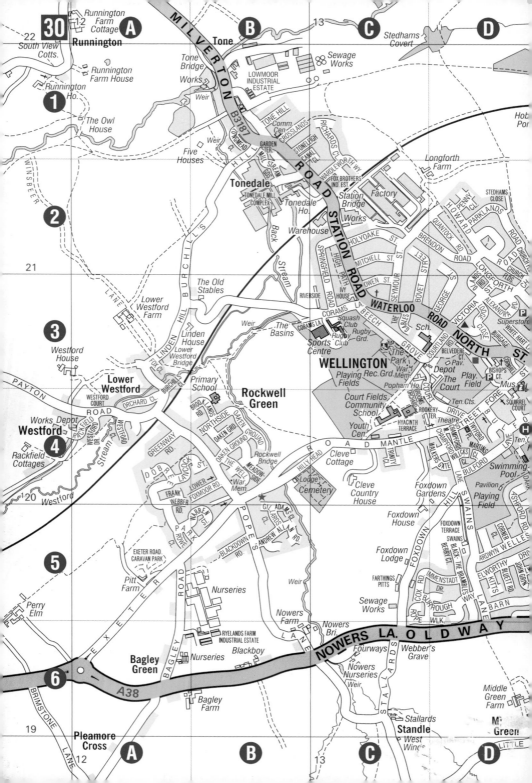

INDEX

Including Streets, Places & Areas, Hospitals & Hospices, Industrial Estates,
Selected Flats & Walkways and Selected Places of Interest.

HOW TO USE THIS INDEX

1. Each street name is followed by its Postal District and then by its Locality abbreviation(s) and then by its map reference;
   e.g. **Acacia Gdns.** TA2: B'pool ....3G **23** is in the Taunton 2 Postal District and the Bathpool Locality and is to be found in square 3G on page **23**. The page number is shown in bold type.

2. A strict alphabetical order is followed in which Av., Rd., St., etc. (though abbreviated) are read in full and as part of the street name;
   e.g. **Black Horse La.** appears after **Blackdown Vw.** but before **Blacklands**.

3. Streets and a selection of flats and walkways too small to be shown on the maps, appear in the index with the thoroughfare to which it is connected shown in brackets; e.g. **Admirals Ct.** TA6: B'wtr....6F **9** (off Quayside)

4. Places and areas are shown in the index in **blue type** and the map reference is to the actual map square in which the town centre or area is located and not to the place name shown on the map; e.g. **Bishops Lydeard** 3B **18**

5. An example of a selected place of interest is **Admiral Blake Mus.** 1G **13**

6. An example of a hospital or hospice is **BRIDGWATER COMMUNITY HOSPITAL** 6G **9**

GENERAL ABBREVIATIONS

& : And	**E.** : East	**Lwr.** : Lower	**St** : Saint
App. : Approach	**Ent.** : Enterprise	**Mnr.** : Manor	**Shop.** : Shopping
Av. : Avenue	**Est.** : Estate	**Mkt.** : Market	**Sq.** : Square
Bldgs. : Buildings	**Fld.** : Field	**Mdw.** : Meadow	**Sth.** : South
Bri. : Bridge	**Flds.** : Fields	**M.** : Mews	**St.** : Street
Bus. : Business	**Gdns.** : Gardens	**Mus.** : Museum	**Ter.** : Terrace
Cvn. : Caravan	**Ga.** : Gate	**Nth.** : North	**Trad.** : Trading
Cen. : Centre	**Grn.** : Green	**Pde.** : Parade	**Up.** : Upper
Circ. : Circle	**Gro.** : Grove	**Pk.** : Park	**Vw.** : View
Cl. : Close	**Ho.** : House	**Pas.** : Passage	**Vs.** : Villas
Cotts. : Cottages	**Ind.** : Industrial	**Pl.** : Place	**Vis.** : Visitors
Ct. : Court	**Info.** : Information	**Res.** : Residential	**Wlk.** : Walk
Cres. : Crescent	**La.** : Lane	**Ri.** : Rise	**W.** : West
Dr. : Drive	**Lit.** : Little	**Rd.** : Road	

LOCALITY ABBREVIATIONS

B Grn : **Bagley Green**	Creech M : **Creech St Michael**	Nails : **Nailsbourne**	Spax : **Spaxton**
B'pool : **Bathpool**	D'ball : **Dunball**	N Curry : **North Curry**	Staple : **Staplegrove**
B'drip : **Bawdrip**	Durl : **Durleigh**	N New : **North Newton**	Stoke M : **Stoke St Mary**
Bish H : **Bishop's Hull**	Durs : **Durston**	N Peth : **North Petherton**	Taun : **Taunton**
Bish L : **Bishops Lydeard**	D'wear : **Dunwear**	Nort F : **Norton Fitzwarren**	Thurl : **Thurlbear**
B'wtr : **Bridgwater**	E Bwr : **East Bower**	P'lett : **Pawlett**	Thurlo : **Thurloxton**
Cann : **Cannington**	Goat : **Goathurst**	Poole : **Poole**	Tone : **Tonedale**
Charl : **Charlynch**	Ham : **Ham**	P'ton : **Puriton**	Trull : **Trull**
Ched F : **Cheddon Fitzpaine**	H'don : **Haydon**	Rhode : **Rhode**	Well : **Wellington**
C'zoy : **Chedzoy**	H'lade : **Henlade**	R Grn : **Rockwell Green**	Wemb : **Wembdon**
C'ston : **Chelston**	H'sey : **Horsey**	R'moor : **Roughmoor**	W Buck : **West Buckland**
Chil T : **Chilton Trinity**	Hunt : **Huntworth**	Ruish : **Ruishton**	West : **Westford**
Comey : **Comeytrowe**	King M : **Kingston St Mary**	R'ton : **Runnington**	W Monk : **West Monkton**
Coss : **Cossington**	Kwle : **Knowle**	R'well : **Runwell**	W'land : **Westonzoyland**
Cotf L : **Cotford St Luke**	Lang : **Langaller**	Samp A : **Sampford Arundel**	Wlvgtn : **Woolavington**
Creech H : **Creech Heathfield**	Monk H : **Monkton Heathfield**	Shore : **Shoreditch**	Wool : **Woolmersdon**

INDEX

A

Acacia Gdns. TA2: B'pool.....3G **23**
Acland Round TA4: Cotf L......6A **18**
Acorn Bus. Cen. TA2: Taun....4G **21**
Adcombe Rd. TA2: Taun 2D **22**
Addison Gro. TA2: Taun 4A **22**
Admiral Blake Mus. 1G **13**
Admirals Ct. TA6: B'wtr............6F **9**
  (off Quayside)
Admiralty Way TA1: Taun 4E **23**
Adscombe Av. TA6: B'wtr.......6A **10**
Albemarle Cen. TA1: Taun 5B **22**
  (off Albemarle Rd.)
Albemarle Rd. TA1: Taun 5B **22**
  TA6: B'wtr.........................1E **13**
Albert Ct. TA1: Taun 6C **22**
  TA6: B'wtr............................1E **13**
Albert St. TA6: B'wtr..............1E **13**
Albion Cl. TA6: B'wtr..............6H **9**
Alder Cl. TA1: Taun................3F **29**
  TA6: N Peth 3E **17**
Alderney Rd. TA6: B'wtr.........2A **14**

Alexander Cl.
  TA3: Creech M.................3C **24**
Alexandra Rd. TA6: B'wtr........6E **9**
  TA21: Well...........................3D **30**
Alexevia Cvn. Pk.
  TA3: Ruish..........................6B **24**
Alfoxton Rd. TA6: B'wtr..........1B **12**
Alfred St. TA1: Taun...............6D **22**
Allen Rd. TA6: B'wtr...............4E **13**
Allerford 5A **20**
Allerton Rd. TA6: B'wtr...........4H **9**
Allington Cl. TA1: Taun 6G **23**
All Saints' Ter. TA6: B'wtr.......1H **13**
Alma St. TA1: Taun 1C **26**
Almond Tree Cl.
  TA6: B'wtr............................1B **14**
Alston Cl. TA1: Taun 3G **27**
Amberd La. TA3: Trull............6G **27**
Amber Mead TA1: Taun..........1F **29**
Amor Pl. TA1: Taun 2H **27**
Andersfield Cl. TA6: B'wtr......1A **12**
Andrew Allan Rd.
  TA21: R Grn 5B **30**

Angela Cl. TA1: Taun 2H **27**
Angel Cres. TA6: B'wtr...........6F **9**
Angel Pl. Shop. Cen.
  TA6: B'wtr............................6F **9**
Anson Way TA6: B'wtr............6F **9**
Apple Bus. Cen.
  TA2: Taun............................4F **21**
Apple Tree Cl. TA6: B'wtr.......1B **14**
Apricot Tree Cl.
  TA6: B'wtr............................6B **10**
Archstone Av. TA5: Chil T......2F **9**
Ardwyn TA21: Well................5D **30**
Arlington Cl. TA6: B'wtr..........3G **13**
Arnold Cl. TA2: Taun 3B **22**
Arundells Way
  TA3: Creech M.....................4B **24**
Arun Gro. TA1: Taun 1F **29**
Ashbourne Cres.
  TA1: Taun............................1F **29**
Ash Cl. TA6: B'wtr.................1B **14**
Ash Cres. TA1: Taun 2F **27**
Ashford 3A **6**
Ashford Cl. TA6: B'wtr...........3E **13**

Ashford Rd. TA1: Taun 2G **27**
  TA21: Well..........................4D **30**
Ash Gro. Way TA6: B'wtr........4B **10**
Ashill Cl. TA1: Taun...............3A **28**
Ashleigh Av. TA6: B'wtr..........2F **13**
Ashleigh Gdns. TA1: Taun.....5A **22**
Ashleigh Ter. TA6: B'wtr.........2F **13**
Ashley Rd. TA1: Taun.............1H **27**
Ashman Way TA1: Taun 1D **12**
Ashton Ct. TA1: Taun..............3G **27**
Ashton Rd. TA6: B'wtr............3F **13**
Aspen Ct. TA6: B'wtr..............1D **12**
Asquith St. TA2: Taun.............3A **22**
Athlone Rd. TA6: B'wtr...........3G **13**
Avalon Rd. TA6: B'wtr.............1B **14**
Avebury Dr. TA6: B'wtr...........6B **10**
Aveline Cl. TA4: Cotf L...........6B **18**
Avenue, The TA1: Taun 5A **22**
  TA6: B'wtr............................6F **9**
  (off High...)
Avon Cl. TA1: Taun.................2H **27**
Axe Rd. TA6: B'wtr.................2F **13**
Aylands Rd. TA1: Taun...........1H **27**

Bacon Dr.—Charlynch La.

B

Bacon Dr. TA1: Taun 1E 29
Badgers Cl. TA1: Bish H 1F 27
Bagborough Dr. TA6: B'wtr 3F 13
Bagborough Rd. TA2: Taun 3B 22
Bagley Green 6A 30
Bagley Rd. TA21: B Grn 6A 30
Baileys Ga. TA4: Cotf L 6A 18
Bailey St. TA6: B'wtr 6H 9
Bakers Cl. TA1: Bish H 1E 27
Baker's La. TA21: Well 3E 31
Baldwin Rd. TA1: Taun 5D 22
Ball's La. TA5: Wool 1C 16
Balmoral Ho. TA6: B'wtr 1A 14
Bannock Drove TA6: P'ton 2A 4
Banwell Cl. TA1: Taun 6F 23
Barbers Mead TA2: Taun 3E 23
Barclay St. TA6: B'wtr 1G 13
Barford Cl. TA5: Spax 6A 6
Barford Rd. TA5: Spax 6A 6
Barhams Cl. TA6: B'wtr 5G 9
Barle Cl. TA1: Taun 6F 23
Barlinch Cl. TA2: Taun 3D 22
Barn Meads Rd.
TA21: Well 5D 30
Barr 5C 20
Barrington Cl. TA1: Taun 4F 27
Barrow Dr. TA1: Taun 5G 23
Barrows Cl. TA6: B'wtr 3E 13
Bartlett Cl. TA1: Taun 3F 27
Barton Cl. TA1: Taun 1H 27
Barton Grn. TA3: Trull 5G 27
Barton Hey TA4: Bish L 3C 18
Barton La. TA3: Ruish 5B 24
Bartons, The TA4: Bish L 2B 18
Batch Cl. TA7: P'ton 3C 4
Batch Rd. TA7: P'ton 1B 4
Bath Bri. Bus. Pk.
TA6: B'wtr 5H 9
Bath Ho. Ct. TA1: Taun 1A 28
Bath Pl. TA1: Taun 1B 28
Bathpool 4G 23
Bathpool La. TA1: Taun 5E 23
Bath Rd. TA6: B'wtr 6H 9
TA7: B'drip, H'sey 5A 10
TA7: Coss, Kwle 1E 11
Batts Pk. TA1: Taun 3H 27
Bawden Cl. TA7: Wlvgtn 4G 5
Bawdrip 1G 11
Bawdrip La. TA7: B'drip 1G 11
Bayford Rd. TA6: B'wtr 5A 10
Baymead Cl. TA6: N Peth 2E 17
Baymead La. TA6: N Peth 3E 17
Baymead Mdw.
TA6: N Peth 3E 17
Baynes Cl. TA21: Well 2E 31
Beadon Rd. TA1: Taun 5E 23
Beauford Cvn. Pk.
TA2: Nort F 4D 20
Beaufort Rd. TA1: Taun 5A 22
Beckworth Cl. TA6: B'wtr 2A 14
Bedford Cl. TA6: B'wtr 2A 14
Beech Ct. TA1: Taun 1A 28
Beech Dr. TA6: B'wtr 6B 10
Beech Gro. TA21: Well 3C 30
Beech Hill TA21: Well 4E 31
Beech Rd. TA6: B'wtr 6B 10
Beechwood TA6: B'wtr 3E 13
Beggs Cl. TA6: N Peth 3E 17
Belgrave Pl. TA2: Taun 4B 22
Bell Cl. TA6: B'wtr 6F 9
Belle Vw. Ter. TA1: Taun 2A 28
Belmont Cl. TA6: B'wtr 1B 12
Belmont Dr. TA1: Taun 2A 28
Belmont Rd. TA1: Taun 1G 27
(in two parts)
Belvedere Cl. TA5: Cann 1F 7
Belvedere Ct. TA21: Well 3D 30
Belvedere Rd. TA1: Taun 5A 22
Belvedere Trad. Est.
TA1: Taun 5A 22
Bernard Taylor Homes
TA1: Taun 6C 22
(off Magdalene St.)
Cl. TA6: B'wtr 3E 13
Berrydale Av. TA6: B'wtr 5F 9
Berwick Cl. TA1: Taun 3G 27
Beverley Cl. TA2: Taun 4A 22
Biddiscombe Cl. TA6: B'wtr 4E 13
Bilberry Gro. TA1: Taun 4D 28
Billetfield TA1: Taun 1B 28
Billet St. TA1: Taun 1B 28
Bincombe Rd. TA6: B'wtr 1A 14
Binding Cl. TA6: N Peth 2E 17
Bindon Rd. TA2: Taun 4F 21
Binford Pl. TA6: B'wtr 6G 9
Bircham Cl. TA6: B'wtr 1C 12
Bircham Rd. TA2: Taun 2D 22
Birch Av. TA7: P'ton 4C 4
Birch Cl. TA5: Cann 2F 7
TA6: B'wtr 6B 10
Birch Gro. TA1: Taun 5A 22
Birch Rd. TA21: Well 4E 31
Bisgood Bldgs. TA6: B'wtr 3A 14
Bishop Fox Dr. TA1: Taun 2C 28
Bishops Ct. TA21: Well 3D 30
Bishop's Hull 6E 21
Bishop's Hull Hill
TA1: Bish H 6F 21
Bishop's Hull Rd.
TA1: Bish H 1E 27
Bishops Lydeard 3B 18
Bishops Lydeard Station 4A 18
(West Somerset Railway)
Bitham La. TA7: Wlvgtn 5F 5
Bitham Wlk. TA7: Wlvgtn 5H 5
Blackberry Ct. TA21: Well 5D 30
Blackbrook Bus. Pk.
TA1: Taun 6G 23
Blackbrook Pk. Av.
TA1: Taun 1G 29
Blackbrook Pavilion
Sports Cen. 2F 29
Blackbrook Rd. TA1: Taun 5G 23
Blackbrook Way TA1: Taun 2F 29
Blackdown Rd. TA2: Taun 2D 22
TA6: B'wtr 1A 14
TA21: R Grn 5B 30
Blackdown Vw.
TA2: Nort F 3D 20
Black Horse La. TA1: Taun 5B 22
Blacklands TA6: B'wtr 6F 9
Blackmoor Rd. TA2: Taun 3D 22
TA21: Well 4E 31
Blackmore La. TA5: Cann 3C 6
Blackthorn Cl. TA6: N Peth 3E 17
Blackthorn Gdns.
TA2: Taun 2C 22
Blagdon Cres. TA1: Taun 3H 27
Blake Gdns. TA6: B'wtr 1G 13
(off St Saviour's Av.)
Blake Ind. Pk. TA6: B'wtr 2G 13
Blake Pl. TA6: B'wtr 6G 9
Blakes La. TA5: Wemb 4C 8
Blakes Rd. TA6: Wemb 4D 8
Blake St. TA1: Taun 6D 22
TA6: B'wtr 1F 13
Blenheim Rd. TA1: Taun 5F 23
TA6: B'wtr 4B 10
Bloomfield Cl. TA1: Taun 6E 23
Bloom Row TA6: B'wtr 6B 10
Blossom Cl. TA6: B'wtr 6A 10
Bluebell Cl. TA1: Taun 4E 29
Bluett Rd. TA21: Well 5D 30
Blythe Ct. TA1: Taun 3H 27
Boards Rd. TA6: B'wtr 5G 9
Bodmin Rd. TA2: Taun 2C 22
Bond St. TA6: B'wtr 6F 9
Boons Orchard TA3: Ruish 6A 24
Booth Way TA6: Wemb 6D 8
Bossington Dr. TA2: Taun 2D 22
Bourne Gro. TA1: Taun 1F 29
Bouverie Rd. TA6: B'wtr 6D 8
Bovet Cl. TA1: Taun 3F 27
Bovet St. TA21: Well 3C 30
Bower Av. TA6: B'wtr 5A 10
Bowerings Rd. TA6: B'wtr 3E 13
Bower La. TA6: E Bwr 4B 10
Bower Mnr. Shop. Cen.
TA6: B'wtr 5B 10
Bowfell Cl. TA1: Taun 3G 27
Bowling Grn. TA5: Cann 1F 7
Bowmont Gro. TA1: Taun 1F 29
Bowood Rd. TA2: Taun 4C 22
Bradbeers TA3: Trull 6G 27
Bradfield Cl. TA6: B'wtr 4E 13
Bradford Cl. TA1: Taun 4G 27
Bradley Green 3E 7
Bradney 3F 11
Bradney La. TA7: B'drip 2D 10
Bramble Pk. TA1: Taun 2E 29
Brambles, The TA21: Well 5D 30
Bramley Rd. TA1: Taun 5F 23
Branksome Av. TA6: B'wtr 6H 9
Brantwood Rd. TA6: Wemb 5C 8
Brendon Rd. TA6: B'wtr 5F 9
TA21: Well 2C 30
Brendons TA4: Bish L 4B 18
Brendon Way TA6: B'wtr 5F 9
Brentsfield La. TA7: C'zoy 1F 15
Brewhouse Theatre &
Arts Cen. 6B 22
Briant Cl. TA1: Taun 3F 27
Bridge St. TA1: Taun 6B 22
Bridge, The TA1: Taun 6B 22
Bridgwater 6F 9
Bridgwater Station 1H 13
Bridgwater Arts Cen. 6F 9
(off Castle St.)
BRIDGWATER COMMUNITY
HOSPITAL 6G 9
Bridgwater Ent. Cen.
TA6: B'wtr 6F 9
Bridgwater Rd. TA1: Taun 6F 23
TA2: B'pool 4G 23
TA6: N Peth 2E 17
Brimstone La.
TA21: Samp A 6A 30
Brindle Cl. TA2: Taun 4G 21
Bristol Rd.
TA6: B'wtr, D'ball 5A 4
Brittons Ash TA2: B'pool 2H 23
Broadguage Bus. Pk.
TA4: Bish L 4A 18
Broadlands Av.
TA6: N Peth 2E 17
Broadlands La. TA5: Durl 1A 12
Broadlands Ri. TA1: Taun 2A 28
Broadlands Rd. TA1: Taun 2A 28
Broadlands Way TA1: Taun 2A 28
Broadlawn TA7: Wlvgtn 4H 5
Broadly Gdns.
TA2: Monk H 1G 23
Broadoak Rd. TA6: B'wtr 6B 10
Broadstone TA7: W'land 5H 15
Broadway TA6: B'wtr 1F 13
Brook Cl. TA6: N Peth 3D 16
Brooke Rd. TA1: Taun 6D 22
Brooklands TA6: B'wtr 6A 10
Brooklands Rd.
TA21: R Grn 4B 30
Brook La. TA5: Cann 2F 7
TA7: B'drip 1H 11
Brookside Cl. TA3: Trull 5H 27
Brooks Pl. TA21: Well 3E 31
Brook St. TA5: Cann 1F 7
TA7: N New 6E 17
Broomfield Ho. TA2: Taun 3A 22
Broughton Cl. TA1: Taun 2E 29
Broughton La.
TA3: Shore, Stoke M 5E 29
Broughton Pk. Res. Homes
TA3: Shore 5F 29
Brownings Rd. TA5: Cann 2F 7
Brue Av. TA6: B'wtr 2G 13
Bruford Cl. TA1: Taun 1A 28
Brunel Ct. TA6: B'wtr 5F 9
(off Waverley Rd.)
Bryer Cl. TA6: B'wtr 4E 13
Brymore Cl. TA6: B'wtr 6D 8
Buces Rd. TA1: Taun 3F 27
Buckingham Cl. TA6: B'wtr 3G 13
Buckland Rd. TA2: Taun 3D 22
Buckwell TA21: Well 3E 31
Bulford TA21: Well 4D 30
Bulford La. TA21: Well 4D 30
Bull Horn Drove
TA7: W'land 5E 15
Bull Mdw. TA4: Bish L 4C 18
Bull St. TA3: Creech M 5C 24
Bungalows, The
TA2: Monk H 1H 23
Burchills Cl. TA21: West 3A 30
Burchill's Hill
TA21: Tone, West 3A 30
Burch's Cl. TA1: Taun 2G 27
Burgage TA21: Well 3D 30
Burge Cres. TA4: Cotf L 6A 18
Burgess Cl. TA1: Taun 3F 27
Burnshill Dr. TA2: Nort F 3E 21
Burns Rd. TA1: Taun 6E 23
Burrough Way TA21: Well 5C 30
Burton Pl. TA1: Taun 1A 28
Bushy Cross La.
TA3: Ruish 6A 24
Bussex 1G 15
Bussex Sq. TA7: W'land 1G 15
Butleigh Cl. TA6: B'wtr 1B 14
Butts Corner TA6: N Peth 2E 17
Byron Rd. TA1: Taun 1E 29

C

Cadeside Cvn. Site
TA21: Poole 2F 31
Calder Cres. TA1: Taun 6F 23
Calvados Rd. TA1: Taun 1E 29
Calway Rd. TA1: Taun 3C 28
Cambridge Ter. TA2: Taun 2C 22
Camden Rd. TA6: B'wtr 6E 9
Campion Dr. TA1: Taun 3E 29
Canal Cl. TA21: Tone 1B 30
Canal Rd. TA1: Taun 5B 22
Canal Ter. TA1: Taun 5B 22
Cannington 1F 7
Cannington Countryside
Vis. Cen. 1F 7
Canns La. TA6: N Peth 2E 17
TA7: P'ton 3C 4
Cann St. TA1: Taun 1A 28
Canon St. TA1: Taun 6B 22
Canworth Way TA6: B'wtr 2A 14
Capes Cl. TA6: B'wtr 6G 9
Caradon Pl. TA6: B'wtr 4F 9
Caray Gro. TA3: Creech M 4C 24
Carlton Dr. TA6: B'wtr 4F 9
Carpenters Cl. TA3: Ruish 6B 24
Carvers Rd. TA6: B'wtr 6G 9
Cashford Ga. TA2: Taun 3E 23
Castle Bow TA1: Taun 6B 22
Castle Cotts. TA21: C'ston 2H 31
Castle Fld. Ind. Est.
TA6: B'wtr 5G 9
Castlefield La.
TA4: Comey 5C 26
Castle Grn. TA1: Taun 6B 22
Castlemans Rd. TA1: Taun 3F 27
Castle Moat TA6: B'wtr 6F 9
Castle Rd. TA21: C'ston 2H 31
Castle Sports Cen., The 6H 21
Castle St. TA1: Taun 6A 22
TA6: B'wtr 6F 9
Castle Wlk. TA1: Taun 6B 22
Castle Way TA1: Taun 6B 22
Cats La. TA2: Ched F 1C 22
Causeway TA7: Wlvgtn 1H 5
Causeway Cl. TA7: Wlvgtn 3H 5
Cecil Ter. TA6: B'wtr 1H 13
Cedar Cl. TA1: Taun 2F 29
TA6: B'wtr 2A 14
Cedar Ct. TA21: Well 4E 31
Celandine Mead TA1: Taun 4E 29
Cellophane Bus. Pk.
TA6: B'wtr 4A 10
Chad's Hill TA5: Cann 1E 7
Chaffinch Cl. TA1: Bish H 6F 21
Chalice M. TA6: B'wtr 6F 9
Chamberlain Ho.
TA1: Taun 5H 21
Chamberlin Av. TA6: B'wtr 5A 10
Champford La. TA21: Well 4D 30
Champford M. TA21: Well 4D 30
Chandos St. TA6: B'wtr 6F 9
Chantry Cl. TA2: Taun 3D 22
Chapel La. TA4: Bish L 2B 18
Chapel St. TA6: B'wtr 1G 13
Chapman Ct. TA1: Taun 3G 27
Charles Cres. TA1: Taun 5F 23
Charlton 2F 25
Charlton Cl. TA6: B'wtr 1A 14
Charlton La. TA3: Creech M 3E 25
Charlton Rd.
TA3: Creech H, Durs 1D 24
Charlynch 5B 6
Charlynch Hill TA5: Charl 5B 6
Charlynch La.
TA5: Cann, Charl 5F 7

Charlynch Rd.
TA5: Charl, Spax..............6A 6
Charnwood Cl. TA6: B'wtr.......4F 9
Charter Wlk. TA1: Taun.......5E 23
Chatham Av. TA6: B'wtr.......5E 9
Chaucer Cl. TA6: N Peth.......2E 17
Cheats Rd. TA3: Ruish.......5A 24
Cheddon Fitzpaine 1E 23
Cheddon M. TA2: Taun.......3B 22
Cheddon Rd. TA2: Taun.......4B 22
Chedzoy 5F 11
Chedzoy La.
TA7: C'zoy, E Bwr.......3C 10
Cheer La. TA7: W'land.......1G 15
Chelmer Cl. TA1: Taun.......6F 23
Chelston 2G 31
Chelston Heathfield 2H 31
Chelston Ter. TA21: C'ston...2H 31
Chelwood Dr. TA1: Taun.......3A 28
Chepstow Av. TA6: B'wtr.......3G 13
Cherry Cl. TA6: B'wtr.......2A 14
Cherry Gro. TA2: Taun.......4B 22
Cherry Orchard TA3: Trull 5H 27
Cherry Tree La. TA1: Taun.....3B 28
Chertsey Cl. TA7: Wlvgtn.......3G 5
Chestnut Cl. TA6: B'wtr.......1A 14
TA21: Well.......4E 31
Chestnut Dr. TA1: Taun.......4E 29
Cheyne Wlk. TA1: Taun.......1B 28
Chidgey Cl. TA6: B'wtr.......6F 9
Chilliswood Cres.
TA1: Taun.......2F 27
Chilliswood La. TA3: Trull....6C 26
Chilpitts TA7: Wlvgtn.......3H 5
Chilton Cl. TA6: B'wtr.......4F 9
Chilton Moor La.
TA6: Chil T 4F 9
Chilton Pk. Res. Cvn. Pk.
TA6: Chil T 4F 9
Chilton Rd. TA5: Chil T 3F 9
TA6: B'wtr, Chil T 4F 9
Chilton St. TA6: B'wtr.......4F 9
Chilton Trinity 2F 9
Chip La. TA1: Taun.......4A 22
(in two parts)
Church Cl. TA2: Nort F.......4D 20
Church Fld. La. TA7: P'ton.....3B 4
(in two parts)
Church Flds. TA21: Well.......2D 30
(in two parts)
Churchill Way TA1: Taun.......2A 28
Church La. TA3: Ruish.......5A 24
TA7: W'land.......2G 15
Church Pas. TA6: B'wtr.......1F 13
(off St Mary St.)
Church Path TA6: B'wtr.......6D 8
Church Rd. TA3: Trull.......5G 27
TA6: Wemb.......5D 8
TA7: B'drip.......1G 11
TA7: N New.......6F 17
Church Sq. TA1: Taun.......6B 22
Church St. TA1: Taun.......1D 28
TA4: Bish L.......2B 18
TA5: Cann.......1F 7
TA6: B'wtr.......6G 9
TA7: Wlvgtn.......3H 5
Church Vw. TA5: Chil T 2F 9
Church Wlk. TA6: N Peth.......3D 16
Claremont Ct. TA1: Taun.......3G 27
Claremont Dr. TA1: Taun.......2F 27
Claremont Gro. TA6: B'wtr....5B 10
Claremont La. TA1: Taun.......3G 27
Clarence Dr. TA6: N Peth.......2E 17
Clarence St. TA1: Taun.......6A 22
Clare St. TA6: B'wtr.......6F 9
(in two parts)
TA6: N Peth.......2E 17
Clark Cl. TA7: Wlvgtn.......4H 5
Clarks Rd. TA6: B'wtr.......1H 13
Cleeve Rd. TA2: Taun.......3D 22
Cleveland St. TA1: Taun.......6A 22
Clifford Ashman Ct.
TA2: Taun.......4A 22
Clifford Av. TA2: Taun.......2A 22
Clifford Cres. TA2: Taun.......2A 22
Clifford Lodge TA5: Cann.....1F 7
Clifford M. TA1: Taun.......3E 31
Clifford Pk. TA5: Cann.......1E 7
Clifford Ter. TA21: Well.......3D 30
Cliff Rd. TA6: N Peth.......4B 9

Clifton Ter. TA2: Taun.......4B 22
Clink, The TA6: B'wtr.......6F 9
Clipper Cl. TA6: B'wtr.......1A 14
Clover Mead TA1: Taun.......4E 29
Cloverton Dr. TA6: B'wtr.......4B 10
Coal Orchard TA1: Taun.......6B 22
Cob Castle TA21: Ham.......2H 31
Cole Cl. TA4: Cotf L.......5A 18
Coleridge Cres. TA1: Taun....1D 28
Coleridge Grn. TA6: B'wtr.....6E 9
(off Coleridge Rd.)
Coleridge Rd. TA6: B'wtr.......5E 9
Coleridge Sq. TA6: B'wtr.......5E 9
Colin Av. TA2: Taun.......2B 22
Colin Rd. TA2: Taun.......3B 22
College Rd. TA2: Taun.......4H 21
College Vw. TA1: Taun.......2G 27
College Way TA1: Taun.......4G 27
TA6: B'wtr.......5H 9
Colley La. TA6: B'wtr.......1H 13
Colley La. Ind. Est.
TA6: B'wtr.......2H 13
Collingwood Ct. TA6: B'wtr 6F 9
(off Drakes Cl.)
Colman Rd. TA1: Taun.......3F 27
Colmer Rd. TA6: B'wtr.......4F 9
Combe La. TA7: Wlvgtn.......4H 5
Comeytrowe 3F 27
Comeytrowe Cen.
TA1: Taun.......3G 27
Comeytrowe Ind. Est.
TA4: Comey.......3E 27
Comeytrowe La. TA1: Taun 3F 27
(nr. Queensway)
TA1: Taun.......2E 27
(nr. Stonegallows)
Comeytrowe Orchard
TA1: Taun.......2E 27
Comeytrowe Ri. TA1: Taun.....2F 27
Comeytrowe Rd. TA1: Taun.....3F 27
TA3: Trull.......3F 27
TA4: Taun, Trull.......3F 27
Compass 6F 13
Compass Hill TA1: Taun.......1A 28
Compass Ri. TA1: Taun.......1A 28
Compton Cl. TA2: Taun.......4C 22
Condell Cl. TA6: B'wtr.......4F 9
Connaught Ho. TA6: B'wtr....6A 10
Conway Rd. TA5: Cann.......1F 7
Cooks Cl. TA3: Creech M.......3C 24
Cook Way TA1: Taun.......4G 21
Coopers Mill TA2: Nort F.......4D 20
Coplestons TA3: Trull.......4H 27
Copper Beeches TA1: Taun 2E 27
Coppin Rd. TA2: Nort F.......4D 20
Copse, The TA6: B'wtr.......6B 10
Corams La. TA21: Well.......3B 30
Corkscrew La.
TA2: Staple, Taun.......2H 21
Cormorant Cl. TA6: B'wtr.......2A 14
Cornborough Pl. TA6: B'wtr 6H 9
Corner Cl. TA21: Well.......5D 30
Cornhill TA6: B'wtr.......1F 13
TA21: Well.......3D 30
Cornishway E. TA1: Taun.......1F 27
Cornishway Nth. TA1: Taun 1F 27
Cornishway Sth. TA1: Taun 2F 27
Cornishway W. TA1: Taun.......1F 27
Coronation Cl. TA3: Ruish.....6B 24
Coronation Ho. TA1: Taun.....5A 10
Coronation Rd. TA6: B'wtr.....6E 9
Corporation St. TA1: Taun.....1B 28
Cory Rd. TA2: Taun.......2C 22
Cossington La.
TA7: Coss, Wlvgtn.......5H 5
Cotford St Luke 6A 18
Cothelstone Cl. TA6: B'wtr 1B 12
Cothelstone Rd.
TA4: Bish L.......1B 18
Cotlake Cl. TA1: Taun.......3B 28
Cotlake Ri. TA1: Taun.......4A 28
County Wlk. TA1: Taun.......1B 28
Court Dr. TA21: Well.......3C 30
Court Gro. TA7: P'ton.......3C 4
Courtland Rd. TA21: Well.......3D 30
Court Orchard TA5: Cann.......2F 7
Court Rd. TA2: Nort F.......4C 20
Court St. TA6: B'wtr.......6F 9
Courtway Av. TA1: Taun.......1A 14

Cowleaze Drove TA3: Ruish...6C 24
Cox Rd. TA21: Well.......5C 30
Crabtrees Cvn. Pk.
TA5: Cann.......1F 7
Craig Lea TA2: Taun.......3A 22
Cranbourne Cl. TA6: B'wtr.....5F 9
Crancombe La.
TA7: Kwle, Wlvgtn.......6F 5
Cranes Cl. TA2: Taun.......3F 23
Cranleigh Gdns.
TA1: Taun.......1G 13
Cranmer Rd. TA1: Taun.......6C 22
Cranwell Cl. TA5: Wool.......1D 16
TA7: W'land.......2H 15
Crawlic La. TA4: Bish L.......1B 18
Creechbarrow Rd.
TA1: Taun.......5E 23
Creechberry Orchard
TA1: Taun.......5F 23
Creech Bus. Pk.
TA3: Creech M.......5B 24
Creech Heathfield 1D 24
Creech Mill Ind. Units
TA3: Creech M.......5B 24
Creech St Michael 4C 24
Creechwood Ter. TA3: Creech M
.......3D 24
Crescent, The TA1: Taun.......1A 28
Crescent Way TA1: Taun.......1B 28
Cresswell Av. TA2: Taun.......3H 21
Crestfield Av. TA6: B'wtr.......4F 9
Crockers Hill TA7: Wlvgtn.....3G 5
Cromwell Rd. TA1: Taun.......5D 22
TA3: Creech M.......3G 13
Crossacre TA6: Wemb.......5D 8
Crossfield Cl. TA6: Wemb.......5D 8
Cross Keys TA2: Nort F.......2E 21
Cross Keys Cl. TA2: Nort F....3E 21
Crosslands TA21: Tone.......1B 30
Crossmead TA7: Wlvgtn.......4H 5
Cross Vw. Ri. TA6: Wemb.......5E 8
Crossway TA1: Taun.......5E 23
Crossways Rd. TA6: B'wtr.....4H 13
Crosswell Cl. TA6: N Peth.....3D 16
Crowcombe Rd. TA2: Taun.....3B 22
Crowcombe Wlk.
TA6: B'wtr.......1C 12
Crown Cl. TA2: Taun.......4E 23
Crown Ind. Est. TA2: Taun.....4E 23
Crown La. TA3: Creech H.......1D 24
Crown Wlk. TA1: Taun.......1B 28
Crowpill La. TA6: B'wtr.......5F 9
Crow's La. TA6: E Bwr.......4C 10
(in two parts)
TA7: E Bwr.......5C 10
Crufts Mdw.
TA3: Creech M.......4B 24
Crypton Technology Bus. Pk.
TA3: Creech M.......4C 24
Culmhead Cl. TA1: Taun.......3H 27
Currymoor Drove
TA3: N Curry.......3H 25
Currypool La. TA5: Cann.......4A 6
Curvalion Gdns.
TA3: Creech M.......4C 24
Curvalion Rd.
TA3: Creech M.......4C 24
Cushuish 1H 19
Cutliff Cl. TA1: Taun.......3A 28
Cypress Dr. TA7: P'ton.......4C 4
Cyril St. TA2: Taun.......4A 22
Cyril St. W. TA2: Taun.......4A 22

D

Dabinett Cl. TA2: Nort F.......3D 20
Dampiet St. TA6: B'wtr.......1F 13
Dancing Hill TA6: N Peth......2B 16
Danesboro Rd. TA6: B'wtr.....1C 12
Darby Way TA4: Bish L.......1C 18
Dare Cl. TA2: Taun.......2C 22
Darkfield Way TA7: Wlvgtn....5G 5
Dark La. TA21: Well.......4D 30
Darwin Cl. TA1: Taun.......3A 28
Davis Cl. TA6: B'wtr.......3F 13
Dawbins Dr. TA7: Wlvgtn.......3H 5
Daws Cl. TA6: B'wtr.......4E 13
Daws La. TA6: N Peth.......4D 16
Daws Mead TA1: Taun.......1E 27

Deacon Rd. TA6: B'wtr.......5A 10
Deal Cl. TA6: B'wtr.......6B 10
Deane Dr. TA1: Taun.......2F 27
Deane Ga. Av. TA1: Taun.......5G 23
Deane Ga. Office Pk.
TA1: Taun.......6G 23
Dellers Ct. TA1: Taun.......5B 22
Deller's Wharf TA1: Taun.......5B 22
Delta Ri. TA4: Bish L.......1B 18
Dene Rd.
TA4: Bish L, Cotf L.......6A 18
Denman's La. TA5: Cann.......2F 7
Denmark Ter. TA2: Taun.......3B 22
Denning Cl. TA1: Taun.......3F 27
Derwent Gro. TA1: Taun.......6F 23
Devonia Pk. Homes
TA3: R'well.......3A 26
Devonshire St. TA6: B'wtr......6H 9
Dillons Rd. TA3: Creech M.....4C 24
Dinhams TA3: Ruish.......5B 24
Dipford 6E 27
Dipford Rd. TA3: Trull.......6E 27
Disraeli Pl. TA1: Taun.......5H 21
Dobree Pk. TA21: R Grn.......4A 30
Dorchester Rd. TA2: Taun.....2C 22
Dorset Rd. TA6: B'wtr.......2A 14
Dosters La. TA2: W Monk.......1A 22
Dover Rd. TA2: Taun.......2C 22
Dovetail Ct. TA1: Taun.......1A 28
Dowell Cl. TA2: Taun.......4G 21
Down End 4A 4
Downend Cres. TA6: B'wtr.....4A 4
Downend Rd. TA6: P'ton.......4A 4
Downend Ter. TA6: P'ton.......4A 4
Downhall Dr. TA6: Wemb.......5D 8
Dowslands 3D 28
Dowsland Way TA1: Taun.......3E 29
Drake Cl. TA2: Taun.......3F 21
Drakes Cl. TA3: Ruish.......5A 24
TA6: B'wtr.......6F 9
Drakes Pk. TA21: Well.......2D 30
Drakes Pk. Nth.
TA21: Well.......2D 30
Drawbridge Ho. TA6: B'wtr....5F 9
Draycott Av. TA2: Taun.......4C 22
Drive, The TA1: Taun.......3H 27
TA7: Wlvgtn.......3H 5
Drove, The TA6: B'wtr.......5G 9
Duke Av. TA5: Cann.......2F 7
Dukes Mead TA6: B'wtr.......3G 13
Duke St. TA1: Taun.......6C 22
Dunball 5A 4
Dunball Drove TA6: D'ball.....4A 4
Dunball Ind. Est.
TA6: D'ball.......4A 4
Duncombe Cl. TA6: B'wtr......6B 10
Dunkerton Ri. TA2: Nort F.....3D 20
Dunkery Rd. TA2: B'wtr.......1C 12
Dunkleys Way TA1: Taun.......3D 22
Dunster Cl. TA2: Taun.......3D 22
Dunwear 3B 14
Dunwear Ho. TA6: B'wtr.......1A 14
Dunwear La. TA6: D'wear......3B 14
Durham Pl. TA2: Taun.......2C 22
Durleigh 2B 12
Durleigh Cl. TA6: B'wtr.......1D 12
Durleigh Hill TA3: Durl.......3A 12
Durleigh Rd. TA6: B'wtr.......1B 12
Durston Way TA1: Taun.......3A 28
Dyers Grn. TA6: N Peth.......3E 17
Dyer's La.
TA6: B'pool, Monk H.......3G 23

E

E. Approach Rd. TA7: P'ton....3F 5
Eastbourne Ct. TA1: Taun.......6C 22
(off Eastbourne Rd.)
Eastbourne Ga. TA1: Taun.....6C 22
Eastbourne Rd. TA1: Taun.....6C 22
Eastbourne Ter. TA1: Taun.....6C 22
East Bower 5B 10
Eastbrook Ter. TA3: Trull......5H 27
Eastern Av. TA6: B'wtr.......1B 14
Eastgate Gdns. TA1: Taun.....6C 22
Eastleigh Rd. TA1: Taun.......1D 28
East Lydeard 2B 18
Eastover 6G 9
Eastover TA6: B'wtr.......6G 9

East Quay—Highfield Cl.

East Quay TA6: B'wtr ... 6G **9**
E. Quay M. TA6: B'wtr ... 5F **9**
East Reach TA1: Taun ... 6C **22**
Eastside La. TA7: B'drip ... 2G **11**
East St. TA1: Taun ... 1B **28**
TA5: Cann ... 1F **7**
Eastwick Av. TA2: Taun ... 3B **22**
Eastwick Rd. TA2: Taun ... 3C **22**
Eastwood Cl. TA6: B'wtr ... 1A **14**
Eaton Cres. TA2: Taun ... 4C **22**
Edgebury TA7: Wlvgtn ... 4H **5**
Edinburgh Rd. TA6: B'wtr ... 3E **13**
Edward St. TA6: B'wtr ... 6H **9**
Eight Acre La. TA21: Well ... 4D **30**
Eldergrove Cl. TA6: B'wtr ... 4B **10**
(off Ash Gro. Way)
Eleven Ct. TA6: B'wtr ... 1E **13**
Elizabeth Ho. TA1: Taun ... 2B **28**
(off Wilton Orchard)
Elizabeth Way TA6: B'wtr ... 1A **14**
Ellen Cl. TA6: N Peth ... 2E **17**
Ellis Gro. TA2: Nort F ... 3C **20**
Elm Gro. TA1: Taun ... 5A **22**
Elmgrove Cl. TA6: B'wtr ... 4B **10**
Elm La. TA7: Wlvgtn ... 4H **5**
Elm Lea Cl. TA7: P'ton ... 4C **4**
Elm Pk. TA1: Taun ... 5A **22**
Elms Cl. TA1: Taun ... 5A **22**
Elms Est. TA2: Monk H ... 2H **23**
Elmside Ho. TA6: B'wtr ... 3F **13**
Elmside Rd. TA6: B'wtr ... 2E **13**
Elms Pde. TA1: Taun ... 5A **22**
Elms Rd. TA21: Well ... 4F **31**
Elm Ter. TA2: Taun ... 4H **21**
Elmwood Av. TA6: B'wtr ... 2F **13**
Elworthy Dr. TA21: Well ... 5D **30**
Enmore Rd. TA2: Taun ... 3B **22**
TA5: Durl ... 2A **12**
Escott Ct. TA6: B'wtr ... 5F **9**
Essex Dr. TA1: Taun ... 3G **27**
Ethpark Gro. TA2: Taun ... 4B **22**
Evesham Dr. TA6: B'wtr ... 4G **13**
Exeter Rd. TA21:
B Grn, R Grn, Well ... 6A **30**
Exeter Rd. Cvn. Pk.
TA21: R Grn ... 5A **30**
Express Pk. TA6: B'wtr ... 2H **9**

F

Fairfax Cl. TA6: B'wtr ... 5A **10**
Fairfax Rd. TA6: B'wtr ... 5A **10**
Fairfield Rd. TA2: Taun ... 2D **22**
Fairwater Cl. TA2: Taun ... 4H **21**
Fairways Camping Site, The
TA7: B'drip ... 6H **5**
Fairways, The TA1: Taun ... 3B **28**
Falcon Ct. TA1: Bish H ... 6G **21**
Farm Vw. TA2: Taun ... 1C **22**
Farrant Cl. TA1: Bish H ... 6E **21**
Farriers Grn. TA2: Monk H ... 3H **23**
Farthing Rd. TA6: B'wtr ... 4E **13**
Farthings Pitts TA21: Well ... 5C **30**
Fennington ... **2G 19**
Fennington La.
TA2: King M ... 3G **19**
Ferndale Dr. TA1: Taun ... 4H **27**
Ferndown Cl. TA1: Taun ... 3H **27**
Fernleigh Av. TA6: B'wtr ... 2F **13**
Feversham Av. TA6: B'wtr ... 5E **9**
Feversham Way
TA2: Taun ... 2D **22**
Field La. TA7: B'drip ... 6G **5**
Fields End TA1: Taun ... 2E **29**
Firepool ... **5C 22**
Firtree Cl. TA6: B'wtr ... 1B **14**
Fitzroy ... **6G 19**
Fivash Cl. TA1: Taun ... 4G **27**
Five Yards TA4: Bish L ... 3C **18**
Fletcher Cl. TA2: Taun ... 2D **22**
Florence Rd. TA2: Taun ... 4B **22**
Folly Cl. TA5: Cann ... 1F **7**
Fons George TA1: Taun ... 2A **28**
(in two parts)
Fons George Cl.
TA1: Taun ... 2A **28**
Fons George Rd.
TA1: Taun ... 2A **28**
Footlands Cl. TA1: Taun ... 3B **28**
Ford St. TA21: Well ... 5F **31**
Fore St. TA1: Taun ... 1B **28**
TA5: Cann ... 1F **7**
TA6: B'wtr ... 6F **9**
TA6: N Peth ... 3D **16**
TA7: W'land ... 5H **15**
TA21: Well ... 4D **30**
Foundry Rd. TA1: Taun ... 6B **22**
Four Acre Mead
TA4: Bish L ... 3C **18**
Fouracres Cl. TA1: Taun ... 3D **28**
Four Forks ... **6A 6**
Four Forks La. TA5: Spax ... 6A **6**
Fowler's Mead Drove
TA7: D'wear ... 4D **14**
Fowler's Plot ... **1F 15**
Fowler St. TA2: Taun ... 4A **22**
Fox Brothers Ind. Est.
TA21: Tone ... 2C **30**
Fox Cl. TA21: West ... 3A **30**
Foxdown Hill TA21: Well ... 5C **30**
Foxdown Ter. TA21: Well ... 5D **30**
Foxhole La.
TA3: Creech M ... 4D **24**
Frampton Rd. TA6: B'wtr ... 3F **13**
Francis Bastin Ho.
TA6: N Peth ... 3D **16**
(off Fore St.)
Francis Cl. TA3: Creech H ... 2D **24**
Francis Reed Cl.
TA7: W'land ... 2G **15**
Francolin Cl. TA1: Taun ... 4A **28**
Franklin Cl. TA2: Taun ... 4F **21**
Franks Cl. TA1: Taun ... 5H **21**
Frank Webber Rd.
TA21: R Grn ... 4A **30**
Frederick Rd. TA6: B'wtr ... 5A **10**
Fremantle Rd. TA1: Taun ... 3D **28**
French Weir Av.
TA1: Taun ... 5A **22**
French Weir Cl. TA1: Taun ... 6A **22**
Frethey Rd. TA4: Bish H ... 6D **20**
Friarn Av. TA6: B'wtr ... 1F **13**
Friarn Lawn TA6: B'wtr ... 1F **13**
Friarn St. TA6: B'wtr ... 1F **13**
Frieze Hill ... **5H 21**
Frobisher Way TA2: Taun ... 4F **21**
Front St. TA7: C'zoy ... 6E **11**
Fry's La. TA7: C'zoy ... 6G **11**
Fullands Av. TA1: Taun ... 4D **28**
Fullands Ct. TA1: Taun ... 3D **28**
Fullands Rd. TA1: Taun ... 3D **28**
Fulwood Cl. TA1: Taun ... 3H **27**
Furlong Grn. TA3: Trull ... 4G **27**
Furlongs Av. TA6: B'wtr ... 3E **13**
Furze Cl. TA6: B'wtr ... 1D **12**

G

Gables, The TA21: Well ... 3C **30**
Galmington ... **2G 27**
Galmington Cl. TA1: Taun ... 1G **27**
Galmington Dr. TA1: Taun ... 2F **27**
Galmington La. TA1: Taun ... 2G **27**
Galmington Rd. TA1: Taun ... 1G **27**
Galmington Trad. Est.
TA1: Taun ... 1F **27**
Garden Ter. TA21: Tone ... 1B **30**
Garden Wlk. TA6: B'wtr ... 3E **13**
Gatchell Grn. TA3: Trull ... 5G **27**
Gatchell Mdw. TA3: Trull ... 5G **27**
Gaunton Cl. TA1: Taun ... 2H **27**
Gay Cl. TA21: Well ... 3E **31**
Gay St. TA21: Well ... 3E **31**
Gelosia Cl. TA7: W'land ... 1G **15**
George St. TA2: Taun ... 4B **22**
(in two parts)
TA6: B'wtr ... 6F **9**
TA21: Well ... 3D **30**
George Williams Ct.
TA6: B'wtr ... 1F **13**
Gerbestone La.
TA21: C'ston, Well ... 6G **31**
Gibb Ho. TA6: B'wtr ... 3E **13**
Gillards TA1: Bish H ... 6F **21**
Gillards Cl. TA21: R Grn ... 5B **30**
Gill Cres. TA1: Taun ... 3F **27**
Gipsy La. TA1: Bish H ... 1G **27**
TA2: Taun ... 3H **21**
Gladstone St. TA2: Taun ... 4A **22**
Gladstone Ter. TA21: Well ... 3E **31**
Glanfield Cl. TA4: Bish L ... 2B **18**
Glasses Mead TA1: Taun ... 3F **27**
Glen Cl. TA2: Nort F ... 2D **20**
Glen Dr. TA2: Taun ... 2C **22**
Glenthorne Rd. TA2: Taun ... 4B **22**
Glenwood Gdns.
TA2: Taun ... 2B **22**
Gloucester Rd. TA6: B'wtr ... 3F **13**
Gloucester St. TA1: Taun ... 6C **22**
Gooch Cl. TA6: B'wtr ... 1H **13**
Gordon Rd. TA1: Taun ... 1C **28**
Gordon's Cl. TA1: Taun ... 3D **28**
Gordon Ter. TA6: B'wtr ... 1G **13**
Gore Sq. TA4: Bish L ... 3B **18**
Gort Rd. TA2: Nort F ... 2C **20**
Gothelney Green ... **6F 7**
Grafton Cl. TA2: Taun ... 2C **22**
Graham Way TA4: Cotf L ... 6A **18**
Granary Way TA3: Trull ... 6H **27**
Grange Cl. TA5: Cann ... 2G **7**
TA21: Well ... 4E **31**
Grange Dr. TA2: Taun ... 4C **22**
TA6: B'wtr ... 2D **12**
Grange Gdns. TA2: Taun ... 3C **22**
Grange Rd. TA2: Taun ... 4C **22**
Grange Walk TA2: Taun ... 4C **22**
Grasmere TA6: Wemb ... 5C **8**
Graves Cl. TA6: B'wtr ... 1H **13**
Grays Av. TA7: W'land ... 4H **15**
Grays Rd. TA1: Taun ... 6D **22**
Great Mead TA1: Bish H ... 1F **27**
Greatwood Cl. TA6: B'wtr ... 4G **13**
Grebe Cl. TA6: B'wtr ... 1H **13**
Grebe Ct. TA6: B'wtr ... 1H **13**
Grebe Rd. TA2: Taun ... 4D **22**
TA6: B'wtr ... 1H **13**
Greenacre TA6: Wemb ... 5D **8**
Greenbrook Ter. TA1: Taun ... 6A **22**
Grn. Dragon Ct. TA6: B'wtr ... 1F **13**
(off Penel Orlieu)
Grn. Dragon La. TA6: B'wtr ... 1F **13**
Greenfield La. TA7: B'drip ... 1F **11**
Greenlands TA1: Taun ... 2D **28**
Green La. TA2: B'pool ... 3A **24**
Green, The TA6: B'wtr ... 3E **13**
Greenway TA2: Monk H ... 2G **23**
TA4: Bish L ... 3A **18**
Greenway Av. TA2: Taun ... 4A **22**
Greenway Cres. TA2: Taun ... 3A **22**
Greenway Rd. TA2: Taun ... 3H **21**
TA4: Bish L ... 4A **18**
TA21: R Grn ... 4A **30**
Grenville Ct. TA6: B'wtr ... 5F **9**
(off Waverley Wharf)
Grenville Ho. TA6: B'wtr ... 3F **13**
(off Rhode La.)
Grenville Vw. TA4: Cotf L ... 6A **18**
Groats TA4: Bish L ... 3C **18**
Grooms Orchard
TA21: Well ... 4C **30**
Grove Dr. TA2: Taun ... 2B **22**
Grove Ter. TA2: Taun ... 4B **22**
Guildford Pl. TA1: Taun ... 1B **28**
Gumbrells Ct. TA6: B'wtr ... 1G **13**
Gurney St. TA5: Cann ... 1G **7**
Gwynne La. TA1: Taun ... 1C **28**
Gyffarde St. TA1: Taun ... 6C **22**

H

Haddon La. TA6: N Peth ... 5A **16**
Hadworthy La. TA6: N Peth ... 6F **13**
Hagget Cl. TA6: B'wtr ... 4F **13**
Haig La. TA2: Nort F ... 1C **20**
Haines Hill ... **2A 28**
Haines Hill TA1: Taun ... 2A **28**
Haines Pk. TA1: Taun ... 3H **27**
Halcon ... **5F 23**
Halesleigh Rd. TA6: B'wtr ... 6D **8**
Hale Way TA2: Taun ... 3F **23**
Hall Rd. TA7: P'ton ... 4B **4**
Halsway TA6: B'wtr ... 6A **10**
Halswell Cl. TA6: B'wtr ... 1E **13**
Ham ... **5F 25**
(nr. Creech St Michael)
Ham ... **1H 31**
(nr. Wellington)
Hamber Lea TA4: Bish L ... 3C **18**
Hamilton Ct. TA1: Taun ... 6E **23**
Hamilton Rd. TA1: Taun ... 6D **22**
Hamlands La. TA21: Ham ... 1H **31**
Ham La. TA7: Wlvgtn ... 3G **5**
Hamlyn Cl. TA1: Taun ... 3G **27**
Hammet St. TA1: Taun ... 6B **22**
TA6: N Peth ... 3D **16**
Hammet's Wlk. TA1: Taun ... 2A **28**
Hammets Wharf TA1: Taun ... 6B **22**
Hamp ... **2F 13**
Hamp Av. TA6: B'wtr ... 2F **13**
Hamp Brook Way
TA6: B'wtr ... 3E **13**
Hamp Grn. Ri. TA6: B'wtr ... 2F **13**
Hamp Ind. Est. TA6: B'wtr ... 2G **13**
Hamp St. TA6: B'wtr ... 2F **13**
Hampton Cl. TA6: B'wtr ... 4B **10**
Hamp Ward TA6: B'wtr ... 2F **13**
Ham Rd. TA3: Creech M ... 5C **24**
TA21: C'ston ... 2G **31**
Hamrod La. TA7: W'land ... 5H **15**
Hamwood TA1: Bish H ... 6F **21**
Hamwood La. TA3: Trull ... 6D **26**
Hankridge Way TA1: Taun ... 5G **23**
Harcourt St. TA2: Taun ... 4A **22**
Hardings Cl. TA6: N Peth ... 3E **17**
Harnell Cl. TA1: Taun ... 1E **29**
Harp Chase TA1: Taun ... 3D **28**
Hartley Way TA1: Taun ... 2F **29**
Hartrow Cl. TA1: Taun ... 3A **28**
Haseley Ct. TA1: Taun ... 2H **27**
(off Ferndown Cl.)
Hatchers Ct. TA2: Taun ... 3B **22**
Hawkers Cl. TA5: Cann ... 2F **7**
Hawker's La. TA5: Cann ... 3F **7**
Hawkridge Rd. TA6: B'wtr ... 1B **12**
Hawthorn Cl. TA6: B'wtr ... 1B **14**
Hawthorne Rd. TA21: Well ... 4E **31**
Hawthorn Rd. TA1: Taun ... 3E **29**
Haydon ... **2F 29**
Haydon Cl. TA1: Bish H ... 6F **21**
Haydon La. TA1: Taun ... 2F **29**
TA3: H'don, H'lade, Taun
... 3D **28**
Haydon Rd. TA1: Taun ... 6C **22**
Haygrove La. TA6: B'wtr ... 2C **12**
Haygrove Pk. Cvn. Pk.
TA3: Trull ... 5H **27**
Haygrove Rd. TA6: B'wtr ... 2C **12**
Hayne La. TA5: Charl, Spax ... 6A **6**
Haywood Rd. TA1: Taun ... 2E **29**
Hazel Cl. TA1: Taun ... 3E **29**
Hazelwood Dr. TA6: B'wtr ... 6C **10**
Healys Mdw. TA4: Cotf L ... 5A **18**
Heathcombe Rd.
TA6: B'wtr ... 1B **12**
Heather Cl. TA1: Taun ... 4E **29**
TA6: B'wtr ... 2H **13**
Heathfield Cl.
TA3: Creech H ... 1D **24**
TA6: N Peth ... 2E **17**
Heathfield Dr.
TA2: Monk H ... 2H **23**
Heavitree Way TA2: Taun ... 4C **22**
Hectors Stones TA7: Wlvgtn ... 3H **5**
Hele ... **1B 26**
Henderson Cl. TA1: Taun ... 2G **27**
(in two parts)
Henley Gro. TA1: Taun ... 1H **27**
Henley Rd. TA1: Taun ... 1H **27**
Herbert St. TA2: Taun ... 4A **22**
Hereford Dr. TA2: Taun ... 2C **22**
Heron Dr. TA1: Bish H ... 6F **21**
Heron Ga. TA1: Taun ... 4G **23**
Heron Ga. Office Pk.
TA1: Taun ... 5G **23**
Heron Ho. TA6: B'wtr ... 1A **14**
Hestercombe Cl.
TA6: B'wtr ... 1B **12**
Hewett Cl. TA1: Taun ... 4G **27**
Highcroft TA7: Wlvgtn ... 4G **5**
Higher Palmerston Rd.
TA1: Taun ... 5H **21**
Higher Poole TA21: Poole ... 1G **31**
Higher Rd. TA7: C'zoy ... 5E **11**
TA7: Wlvgtn ... 3G **5**
Highfield TA1: Bish H ... 1G **27**
TA1: Taun ... 2E **27**
Highfield Cl. TA1: Taun ... 2E **27**

A-Z Taunton 35

Highfield Cres.—Manor M.

Highfield Cres. TA1: Taun 2E **27**
Highgrove TA1: Taun 3A **28**
Highgrove Cl. TA6: B'wtr 3G **13**
Highlands TA1: Taun 3A **28**
High Path TA21: Well 2C **30**
High St. TA1: Taun 1B **28**
TA4: Bish L 2B **18**
TA5: Cann 2E **7**
TA5: Spax 6A **6**
TA6: B'wtr 1F **13**
TA6: N Peth 3D **16**
TA21: Well 3D **30**
Hilary Rd. TA1: Taun 1H **27**
Hilda Coles Ho. TA6: B'wtr 1F **13**
(off Albert St.)
Hillgrove Cl. TA6: B'wtr 6E **9**
Hill Head Cl. TA1: Taun 1C **28**
Hillsboro TA7: Wlvgtn 4H **5**
Hillside TA7: P'ton 4C **4**
Hillside Cres. TA7: P'ton 4C **4**
Hillside Dr. TA7: P'ton 4C **4**
Hillside Gro. TA1: Taun 2G **27**
Hill Ter. TA1: Bish H 6E **21**
Hillyfields TA1: Taun 2E **29**
Hilly Head TA21: Well 4B **30**
Hilly Pk. TA2: Nort F 3C **20**
Hine Rd. TA1: Taun 3F **27**
Hinton Dr. TA1: Taun 3A **28**
Hither Mead TA4: Bish L 3B **18**
Hobbs Mead TA4: Bish L 3C **18**
Holford Rd. TA2: Taun 2A **22**
TA6: B'wtr 1A **12**
Hollow La. TA6: Wemb 5C **8**
Holly Cl. TA1: Taun 3E **29**
TA6: B'wtr 6C **10**
TA6: N Peth 3E **17**
Holway **2E 29**
Holway TA6: N Peth 2F **17**
Holway Av. TA1: Taun 1C **28**
Holway Deane TA1: Taun 2F **29**
Holway Grn. TA1: Taun 2E **29**
Holway Hill TA1: Taun 1D **28**
Holway Rd. TA1: Taun 1D **28**
Holyoake St. TA21: Well 2C **30**
Homecastle Ho. TA6: B'wtr 6F **9**
Home Cotts. TA1: Taun 5H **21**
(off Roseberry Ter.)
Homefield TA21: Well 5E **31**
Homefield Cl.
TA3: Creech M 4C **24**
Honiton Rd. TA3: Trull 6G **27**
Hoopers Cl. TA1: Taun 2F **27**
Hope Corner Cl.
TA2: Taun 2A **22**
Hope Corner La.
TA2: Taun 2A **22**
Hornbeam Cl. TA1: Taun 2F **29**
TA6: B'wtr 6B **10**
Horner Rd. TA2: Taun 3D **22**
Horsepond La. TA6: B'wtr 1F **13**
Horsey **2C 10**
Horsey La.
TA6: B'wtr, H'sey 1A **10**
(in three parts)
TA7: H'sey 1B **10**
(in two parts)
Horton Way TA7: Wlvgtn 4G **5**
Horts Rd. TA1: Taun 3G **27**
Hoveland Cres. TA1: Taun 2H **27**
Hoveland Dr. TA1: Taun 3H **27**
Hoveland La. TA1: Taun 2G **27**
Hovelands Ct. TA1: Taun 2H **27**
Howard Rd. TA21: Well 2D **30**
Howell's La. TA6: Thurlo 6B **16**
Hoyles Cl. TA21: Well 5E **31**
Hoyles Rd. TA21: Well 5E **31**
Hudson Way TA2: Taun 4F **21**
Hughes Cl. TA6: B'wtr 1H **13**
Hugo St. TA1: Taun 6C **22**
Huish Cl. TA1: Taun 6F **23**
Hulkshay La. TA6: N Peth 3C **16**
Humber Gro. TA1: Taun 1F **29**
Humphreys St. TA21: Well 2E **31**
Huntworth **6A 14**
Huntworth Bus. Pk.
TA6: B'wtr 5H **13**
Huntworth La. TA6: N Peth 1F **17**
TA7: Hunt 1G **17**
Hurdle Way TA1: Taun 1C **28**
Hyacinth Ter. TA21: Well 4C **30**
Hyde La. TA2: B'pool 4G **23**
TA3: Creech M 3A **24**
Hyde La. Cotts.
TA2: B'pool 3A **24**
Hyde La. Pk. TA2: B'pool 4G **23**
Hyde Pk. TA6: N Peth 3D **16**
Hyde Pk. Av. TA6: N Peth 3D **16**
Hylton Cl. TA2: Taun 2B **22**

I

Ilford Ct. TA1: Taun 2G **27**
(off Wiltshire Cl.)
Ilminster Rd. TA1: Taun 6F **23**
Immenstadt Dr.
TA21: Well 5D **30**
Improvement Pl.
TA21: Well 4D **30**
(off Bulford La.)
Inner Circ. TA1: Taun 5F **23**
Inner Gullands TA1: Taun 1H **27**
Inwood Rd. TA6: Wemb 6C **8**
Irene Cl. TA6: B'wtr 4B **10**
Irvine Cl. TA2: Taun 4G **21**
Irwell Grn. TA1: Taun 6F **23**
Ivors Way TA6: N Peth 2D **16**
Ivy Gro. Cl. TA6: B'wtr 4B **10**
Ivy Ho. TA21: Well 3C **30**

J

Janson Cl. TA6: B'wtr 5B **10**
Japonica Cl. TA6: B'wtr 6B **10**
Jarmyns TA1: Bish H 1E **27**
Jeffreys Way TA1: Taun 2D **26**
Jellalabad Ct. TA1: Taun 1B **28**
John Grinter Way
TA21: Well 5D **30**
Jubilee Cl. TA6: B'wtr 1A **14**
Jubilee St. TA2: Taun 4A **22**
Judy's Orchard
TA7: W'land 2G **15**
Juniper Cl. TA6: B'wtr 1C **14**
Juniper Rd. TA1: Taun 2E **29**
Jurston La. TA21: Well 3E **31**
(in three parts)

K

Keats Rd. TA1: Taun 1E **29**
Keltings TA6: Wemb 5C **8**
Kelway Rd. TA21: Well 2E **31**
Kendale Rd. TA6: B'wtr 6E **9**
Kendall Cl. TA3: Creech H 1D **24**
Kennet Gro. TA1: Taun 6F **23**
Kensington Gdns.
TA6: B'wtr 5B **10**
Kent Av. TA6: B'wtr 3G **13**
Kenwyn Cl. TA1: Taun 1F **29**
Kestrel Cl. TA6: B'wtr 2A **14**
Kidsbury Rd. TA6: B'wtr 5E **9**
Kilburn Dr. TA6: B'wtr 5B **10**
Kilkenny Av. TA2: Taun 4B **22**
Kilkenny Ct. TA2: Taun 4B **22**
Killams Av. TA1: Taun 5D **28**
Killams Cl. TA1: Taun 4D **28**
Killams Cres. TA1: Taun 4D **28**
Killams Dr. TA1: Taun 4D **28**
Killams Grn. TA1: Taun 4D **28**
Killams La. TA1: Taun 4D **28**
TA3: Shore 6C **28**
Kilmorie Cl. TA1: Taun 2G **27**
Kilve Cl. TA2: Taun 3B **22**
Kilve Cres. TA2: Taun 3B **22**
Kimberley Ter. TA6: B'wtr 4H **9**
Kinders Cl. TA7: Wlvgtn 4H **5**
King Alfred Cl.
TA6: N Peth 2E **17**
Kingdom La. TA2: Nort F 4D **20**
Kingdon Mead
TA3: Creech M 4C **24**
Kingfisher Cl. TA6: B'wtr 2A **14**
King George Av. TA6: B'wtr 3F **13**
King's Castle Bus. Est.
TA6: B'wtr 5G **9**
Kingscliffe Ter. TA6: B'wtr 3G **13**
Kings Cl. TA1: Taun 2C **28**
Kingsdown Cl. TA6: B'wtr 5B **10**
Kings Dr. TA7: W'land 5H **15**
Kingsley Cl. TA1: Taun 3G **27**
King's Pl. TA6: B'wtr 6F **9**
King Sq. TA6: B'wtr 6F **9**
Kingston Cl. TA2: Taun 3A **22**
Kingston Rd. TA2:
Nails, Staple, Taun 1A **22**
King St. TA6: B'wtr 6F **9**
Kingsway TA1: Taun 4D **28**
Kirk Dr. TA7: W'land 4H **15**
Kirke Gro. TA2: Taun 2D **22**
Kitchener Rd. TA2: Nort F 1B **20**
Kitts TA21: Well 5D **30**
Knapp **4H 25**
Knapp Rd. TA3: N Curry 5G **25**
Knightsbridge Way
TA6: B'wtr 5B **10**
Knights Rd. TA21: C'ston 2H **31**
Knoll Grn. La. TA5: Cann 2A **6**
Knowle **1F 11**
Knowle End TA7: Wlvgtn 5H **5**
Knowle Rd. TA6: B'wtr 5A **10**

L

Laburnum Cl. TA6: B'wtr 1B **14**
Laburnum Ct. TA1: Taun 6C **22**
(off Laburnum St.)
Laburnum Rd. TA21: Well 4E **31**
Laburnum St. TA1: Taun 6C **22**
Laburnum Ter.
TA3: Creech M 4C **24**
La Ciotat Ho. TA6: B'wtr 1G **13**
Ladylawn TA3: Trull 5H **27**
Ladymead Cl. TA6: B'wtr 1B **12**
Ladymead Rd. TA2: Taun 1B **22**
Lakeside Pk. TA6: B'wtr 2G **13**
Lamb La. TA6: B'wtr 1F **13**
Lambrook Cl. TA1: Taun 6D **22**
Lambrook Rd. TA1: Taun 5D **22**
Lambrook Way TA1: Taun 6E **23**
Lancock St. TA21: R Grn 4A **30**
Langaller **2B 24**
Langaller La. TA2: B'pool,
Creech M, Lang 1A **24**
TA3: Creech M 1A **24**
Langford **2D 20**
Langford La. TA2: Nort F 2D **20**
Langham Dr. TA1: Taun 3G **27**
Langham Gdns. TA1: Taun 3G **27**
Langmoor Drove
TA7: W'land 3H **15**
Lansdowne Rd. TA2: Taun 4C **22**
Larch Cl. TA1: Taun 2F **29**
TA6: B'wtr 5B **10**
Larkspur Cl. TA1: Taun 3E **29**
Larkspur Ct. TA2: Taun 3H **21**
Laurel Cl. TA1: Taun 2E **29**
Laurels, The TA6: Wemb 5C **8**
Lavender Gro. TA1: Bish H 1G **27**
Laverock Ct. TA1: Taun 5A **22**
Lawn Mdw. TA3: Ruish 6B **24**
Lawn Rd. TA2: Staple 2G **21**
Laxton Cl. TA1: Taun 5F **23**
Laxton Rd. TA1: Taun 5F **23**
Leadon Gro. TA1: Taun 1F **29**
Leafield Cl. TA2: Nort F 3C **20**
Leat, The TA4: Bish L 3C **18**
Leeward Cl. TA6: B'wtr 1A **14**
Leggar, The TA6: B'wtr 6G **9**
Leigh Rd. TA2: Taun 2D **22**
Leonard Houlder Ct.
TA2: Taun 2C **22**
Leslie Av. TA2: Taun 4A **22**
Lethbridge Pk. TA4: Bish L 2A **18**
Lewis Rd. TA2: Taun 3A **22**
Leycroft Cl. TA1: Taun 6D **22**
Leycroft Gro. TA1: Taun 6D **22**
Leycroft Rd. TA1: Taun 6D **22**
Leyton Dr. TA6: B'wtr 5B **10**
Liberty Pl. TA6: B'wtr 1H **13**
Lilac Cl. TA1: Taun 2E **29**
Lillebonne Cl. TA21: Well 3E **31**
Lime Cres. TA1: Taun 2E **29**
Limestone Hill TA5: Cann 4G **7**
Lime Tree Cl. TA6: B'wtr 1B **14**
Linden Cl. TA6: B'wtr 1A **14**
Linden Gro. TA1: Taun 5A **22**
Linden Hill TA21: West 3A **30**
Lindsey Cres. TA6: N Peth 3E **17**
Liney **1H 15**
Liney Rd. TA7: W'land 1H **15**
Linham Rd. TA6: B'wtr 5F **9**
Linley Cl. TA6: B'wtr 4B **10**
Linnet Cl. TA1: Bish H 6F **21**
Lipe Hill La. TA4: Comey 6C **26**
TA21: Comey, W Buck 6C **26**
Lipe La. TA3: H'lade, Ruish 6B **24**
Lisieux Ct. TA1: Taun 2F **29**
Lisieux Way TA1: Taun 6E **23**
Little Cl. TA2: Staple 2G **21**
Little Mdw. TA4: Bish L 3C **18**
Lit. Silver La. TA21: Well 6D **30**
Lit. Wall La.
TA7: B'drip, Kwle 1F **11**
Livingstone Way TA2: Taun 4F **21**
Lloyd Cl. TA1: Taun 3F **27**
Load La. TA7: W'land 5H **15**
Lockswell TA7: Wlvgtn 3H **5**
Lodge Cl. TA1: Taun 2E **27**
TA21: Well 3D **30**
Longacre Cl. TA2: Taun 3A **22**
Longacre Drove TA7: C'zoy 1E **15**
Longforth Rd. TA21: Well 2D **30**
Long La. TA2: Lang 1C **24**
Longmead Cl. TA1: Taun 2H **27**
TA21: Tone 1B **30**
Longmead Way TA1: Taun 2H **27**
Longrun La. TA1: Bish H 5G **21**
Longstone Av. TA6: B'wtr 1A **14**
Lonsdale Rd. TA5: Cann 2F **7**
Lovers' Wlk. TA5: Cann 2E **7**
Lwr. Bath Rd. TA6: B'wtr 5H **9**
Lwr. Foxmoor Rd.
TA21: R Grn 4B **30**
Lwr. Holway Cl. TA1: Taun 2F **29**
Lwr. Middle St. TA1: Taun 6B **22**
Lower Rd. TA7: Wlvgtn 3G **5**
Lower Westford **3A 30**
Lowlands Ter. TA1: Bish H 6F **21**
Lowmoor Ind. Est.
TA21: Tone 1B **30**
Loxleigh Av. TA6: B'wtr 1H **13**
Loxleigh Gdns. TA6: B'wtr 1H **13**
Loxley Ter. TA6: B'wtr 4F **9**
Ludlow Av. TA2: Taun 2C **22**
Ludlow Cl. TA6: B'wtr 3G **13**
Luttrell Cl. TA2: Taun 2D **22**
Luxborough Rd. TA6: B'wtr 1A **12**
Luxhay Cl. TA2: Taun 2D **22**
Lyddon Cl. TA21: Well 5D **30**
Lydeard Mead TA4: Bish L 3B **18**
Lyndale Av. TA6: B'wtr 6E **9**
Lyndhurst Cres. TA6: Wemb 6C **8**
Lyngford **4C 22**
Lyngford Cres. TA2: Taun 3C **22**
Lyngford La.
TA2: Ched F, Taun 2C **22**
Lyngford Pl. TA2: Taun 3C **22**
Lyngford Rd. TA2: Taun 4C **22**
Lyngford Sq. TA2: Taun 3C **22**
Lynor Cl. TA1: Taun 1F **29**

M

Maddocks Ct. TA6: B'wtr 5F **9**
(off Waverley Wharf)
Magdalene La. TA1: Taun 6B **22**
Magdalene St. TA1: Taun 6B **22**
Magnolia Tree Rd.
TA6: B'wtr 6C **10**
Maidenbrook La.
TA2: Ched F 1E **23**
Main Rd. TA5: Cann 2F **7**
TA7: W'land 2G **15**
Mallard Way TA6: B'wtr 1G **13**
Mallory Cl. TA2: Taun 4F **21**
Malthouse Ct. TA1: Bish H 6E **21**
Malvern Cl. TA6: B'wtr 5B **10**
Malvern Ter. TA2: Taun 4B **22**
Mandarin Cl. TA6: B'wtr 1H **13**
Manning Rd. TA4: Cotf L 5A **18**
Manor Cl. TA1: Taun 2A **28**
Manor Dr. TA1: Taun 1A **28**
TA2: Staple 3G **21**
TA7: C'zoy 5F **11**
Manor M. TA2: Staple 2H **21**